C000242597

ALL ABOUT BEER

ALL ABOUT BEER

by

BOB PRITCHARD

The brewing process described and reduced to home brewing terms, enabling anyone to brew really good beer with minimum effort.

Published by

Amateur Winemaker Publications

Argus Books Limited
1 Golden Square
London W1R 3AB
England

© Argus Books 1984

First Published 1983
Reprinted 1986

ISBN 0 900841 72 9

All rights reserved.
No part of this publication
may be reproduced in any form
without written permission
from Argus Books Ltd.

**All Photographs by: The Author except those of the Berkshire
brewery which are by courtesy of Courage Ltd.**

Printed in Great Britain by
The Garden City Press Limited,
Letchworth, Hertfordshire SG6 1JS.

Contents

CHAPTER 1

Barley and Malt

The making of an alcoholic drink or ale from barley reaches back into antiquity and records show that it occurred in the Sumerian civilisation in the valley of the Tigris and Euphrates before the emergence of ancient Egypt.

The drink has invariably been made by the fermentation of sugars extracted from barley, as this cereal was the indigenous crop grown throughout Egypt and Mesopotamia long before the cultivation of wheat, oats and maize.

In Britain ale made from barley has always been the staple drink, mainly because Britain is a cereal-growing country rather than a grape-growing country.

The ale was often flavoured with herbs; it was not until the 15th century that hops were introduced from the Low Countries and Germany and the drink became the hopped beer we know today.

It is not altogether true to say that ale became beer when hops were added, because early Celtic barley was known as "bere" or "beere" and so probably gave the name to beer. Confusion can still arise, as modern breweries call their best bitter beer 'India Pale Ale' and an abbreviation of this to 'I.P.A.' is often a brewery's inexpensive, low gravity beer.

However, the general name for the drink, be it bitter, light, mild or dark, is BEER.

Barley is the main alcohol-yielding ingredient of beer but it is of no use to the brewer as grain harvested from the farm. It is insoluble in hot or cold water and will not yield the fermentable sugars in the easy way that a grape does – simply by crushing out the readily fermentable juice for the bloom on the grape, which will have some yeast present, to break down into wine. This was a very simple process for ancient people to stumble upon.

BARLEY CORN

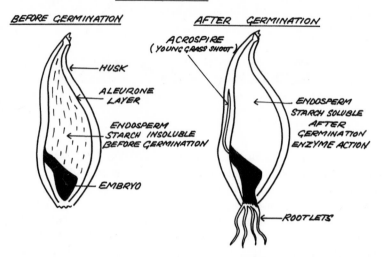

Barley corns, which are the seed of the barley plant, have to be germinated or 'sprouted' and only then will the starch in the centre of the corn 'modify' or break down into the more simple starches which will liquify into sugars with hot water.

One can only assume that people centuries ago discovered this by accident. Perhaps some barley stored in some sort of container became damp enough to germinate and before the now 'modified' starch in the corn was used up by growth of the new plant some warm water was added which caused a conversion to fermentable sugars. Wild yeast, which is always present in air, might have fallen on to the liquid and broken it down into an alcoholic drink, with the usual beneficial result!

Once it was discovered that only germinated barley produced this result, it follows that those past generations would deliberately germinate some of their crop and then dry it off to stop full growth and enable them to store it until such time as they wanted, then crush and mix it with hot water and allow to ferment.

The Fellaheen, or peasants, of Egypt, to this day allow barley to germinate in large pots and then crush the sprouted barley, with the addition of some dough containing yeast. Loaves are shaped from this and baked in such a way that the interior remains unbaked.

When required, the loaves are broken up in warm water and the yeast from the dough ferments the liquid into the drink called 'boozah'. Early English soldiers in Egypt brought this word back and it became our word 'booze'.

Through the centuries, therefore, beer has been brewed from barley but the barley must first be germinated, then the growth stopped by drying (kilning). After the now dry embryo rootlets are screened away, the modified barley corns, now called malt, can be stored until required.

The brewer takes this malt, lightly crushes it and mashes it with hot water; the modified starch of the malt converts to sugars which are washed out and boiled with hops and this solution is cooled and fermented by yeast, into beer.

The production of malt from barley appears to be a fairly simple process, but it is extremely complex and whole volumes have been written by biologists and scientists who have researched the subject. I will only touch on the broad outlines.

Any cereal grain can be malted but barley (Hordeum Sativum), while being randomly selected in the beginnings of brewing, is in fact particularly suited to malting, as the husk adheres to the corn after threshing and this, unlike other cereals, allows the seed leaf or acrospire to grow up under this protective husk during germination, avoiding damage during the handling and movement of large amounts of grain.

The barley corn is the fruit and seed of the barley plant and consists of an outer layer or husk and then the corn proper, called the aleurone layer; within this is the store of starch called the endosperm, whose real job is to provide early plant food for the embryo that lies at the base of the corn. The starch is not soluble and convertible to sugar at this stage, because it is enclosed in a complex cellulose structure.

When barley is wetted and put in a suitable temperature, germination and growth will start. Nobody knows precisely what prompts plant or animal growth or life, but once it has started, enzymes take over. Enzymes are naturally-occurring activating agents in plants and animals, which trigger off digestion, respiration and all metabolic processes.

Knowledge of enzyme action was only beginning at the end of the 19th century but in the last 80 years tremendous strides have been made in the understanding and isolation of hundreds of enzymes acting and interacting in all biochemical changes and throughout the whole process of malting, mashing and fermenting beer.

When I started brewing, some 40 years ago, cytase was the enzyme considered to be the agent in breaking down the cellulose structure in the sprouting barley corn, but today it is realised that several enzymes, such as protease to break down cellulose, amylase to begin to solubilise the starch, and glucanase to absorb barley gums all play their part.

The growth in the corn is allowed to go on until small rootlets develop and the acrospire (infant blade of grass) has grown to about half the length of the corn; in barley, this grows under the husk. The modification of the starch has now taken place and growth is stopped by kilning. This drying process is not too severe, as enzymes have to be retained in the malt, as the grain is now called, for final saccharification of the modified starch in the brewery mashing process (as we shall see later).

Malting has now become an engineering operation, concerned with carrying out the process in huge quantities. These bulk methods have been brought about by the disappearance of hundreds of small maltings and small breweries, to form the great malting and brewery groups of today.

There are several systems, but all are merely different engineering solutions for carrying out the process by bulk handling and movement of the grain with as little labour as possible and with full control over temperatures of steeping, humidity and heat of germination and kilning.

Types of malt are determined in the main by time of germination and various degrees of kilning, coupled with a comparatively slight variation in original barley quality.

MALTING AT HOME

Many keen home-brewers like to do their own malting at home and it is fairly simple to handle about five pounds of barley to make later into five gallons of beer. Buy clean, rounded-grain barley and first test a dozen or so corns for germination. Put them in water for a day, then lay them between blotting paper in the airing cupboard where they should sprout after seven or eight days.

If the test has worked, steep all the barley in a bucket with water at about 60°F for 48 hours, changing the water about four times. Lay out the wet barley inside newspapers, at a temperature of about 60/65°F. Do not let the grain dry out; keep it just damp. Germination should start in seven or eight days. Allow this to proceed until you can see the acrospire showing as a slight shape half-way up the husk. Transfer to trays and kiln gently at 120°F for 12 hours in an oven with door open and turn the grains from time to time. Do not overdry, as this will destroy enzymes needed for conversion to sugar when you mash later in the brewing operation.

1. Mashing at home: ground malt being poured into required amount of hot water at about 160°F.

CHAPTER 2

The Brewery Mash

When I refer to "malt" it is always to malt as grain. I mention this because many people identify "malt" as a sticky brown syrup. This is a concentrated *extract* of malt which will be discussed later.

Malt is the heart and soul of beer and the mash tun is the heart and soul of any brewery; in the mash tun the type and character of the beer is decided. Superficially, it is an extremely simple process. The brewer, the day before mashing, will have decided on the quantity and type of malt required. This will have been milled lightly, so that the husk of the malt is just cracked open to expose the malt flour. This, now known as 'grist', is held in a container above the mash tun.

Before the days of machinery the mash tun was an open-topped, round wooden vessel with one or two holes in the bottom covered by metal strainers, leading to taps under the vessel. At the beginning of the brew the tun would be half filled with hot water ("liquor", as brewers call it) at about 168°F and the grist would be tipped into this and mashed with oars and rakes into a porridge-like consistency.

The temperature of the mash (or 'goods' as brewers say) would now be about 150°F. The ratio of malt grist to water would be about 4 lbs of grist to one gallon of water. Home brewers who mash should use this yardstick.

The mash is now allowed to 'stand on' for about two hours, during which time the starch will liquefy into fermentable sugars.

The taps are now progressively opened, to allow the sugars to flow into a vessel where they will be boiled with hops. At the same time, water at about 170°F is sprayed, or 'sparged' on to the surface of the mash. The husks of the malt make their own filter bed so that only liquid sugars are washed out of the tun. This liquid is now called 'wort' (pronounced 'wurt').

It is desirable to use as little sparge as possible, to obtain full extraction of sugars without extracting colloidal and protein matter that would cause haze problems later in the beer process. Homebrew mashers should find half a gallon per lb of grist enough to obtain full extraction.

The chemistry of mashing is complex but mechanically it is simply a temperature-controlled mixing and filtration operation.

As breweries grew larger, mash tuns were improved and became large, cast iron vessels, insulated to conserve mash heat and with a false bottom of filter plates an inch or two above the base.

The new tuns had more 'spend' pipes connected to taps, to draw off wort more evenly. The grist was mechanically mixed with water, into the tun, and sparging was carried out by revolving arms spraying the surface of the mash.

The mash has to be operated with some care, to obtain filtration through the husks of the 'goods'. Setting the draw-off taps too far open pulls the mash down and it will 'set' solidly; too much sparge and the mash will flood. The aim is for the mash to be almost floating in the throughput of water, enabling efficient leaching out of the sugars for maximum extraction.

This has led many homebrewers to imitate the mashing method with vessels and watering cans for sparging in the belief that these are essential to produce good beer. But it is only the limitations of the mash tun that require this.

The general requirement at home and in breweries, is the quickest method of extracting the sugars from the husks and, over the last 20 years, the big breweries have adopted better methods for large quantities.

From Germany came the valley bottom Lauter tun. This is an improved mash tun, of large area, with a wire type of filter, to hold back husks. The mash is made up in a separate vessel, where saccharification takes place in about one hour. The mash is then pumped into the Lauter tun and levelled off to make a very shallow bed of grain. A high rate of sparge is applied to this and the sugars are rapidly washed out of the shallow bed of mash into the valley-shaped bottom where they run away freely into the hopping and boiling vessel.

Next, from Belgium, came the 'Strainmaster' system. Again the mash saccharifies in a separate vessel and is then pumped into the

14

Strainmaster. This is a large, closed, cylindrical vessel with a great number of perforated tubes arranged inside in the fashion of a steam tubed boiler. These are all linked in to a pump which literally sucks the sugars from the mash. Internal sparging is also incorporated.

Centrifugal separation has also been used and currently many breweries are going over to mechanical pressure mash filters.

Brewers will 'stop taps' when the gravity of the wort is 1.002 as, beyond that, haze forming cyanogens from malt husk would start dissolving out into the last runnings of the mash.

The above is known as the INFUSION system of mashing used by all British ale brewers and it is a simple and unsophisticated operation but is not like making a cup of instant coffee.

In all mashing operations, the conversion and liquefying of the malt starch is brought about by the barley enzymes carefully preserved in the malting process. When the ground malt mixes with hot water at the initial heat of the mash, about 150°F, a series of enzymes start their work of digestion. These are given the general name of *diastase* but this is made up of many different enzymes.

The starch can be visualised as chains; *beta amylase* first chops these into smaller lengths; *alpha amylase* breaks these down into maltose and glucose and another enzyme, *dextrinase*, produces a small amount of dextrinous sugar.

Variations in proportions of the sugars can be achieved by temperature control, to activate or inhibit enzyme action. High mash temperatures will check amylase action and produce more slowly fermenting dextrin and low mash temperatures encourage formation of freely fermenting maltose. In the main, however, a normal mash produces a wort with a composition as follows:–

60% maltose
2% glucose
6% sucrose
7% dextrin
5% nitrogenous protein
20% dry residue

This wort contains all the necessary sugars and yeast feeding proteins to ferment with yeast into beer, after adjusting to the required gravity, boiling with hops, and cooling.

I hope the home masher now sees that there are two requirements. One – conversion of malt starch to sugars. Two – separation of these sugars from the husks.

CONVERSION

I use a large aluminium jam boiling pan and make up the mash, with lightly crushed malt, at about 150°F. I put this in a very low oven, with the door open, for 1½ hours, to maintain the temperature, and stir the mash once or twice to assist conversion.

2.   **Stir mash thoroughly.**

3.   **Check temperature of mash. If not 150°F mash may be heated gently on gas burner while being stirred.**

4. **Place mash in a warm oven with door open for 1½ hours. Stir once or twice.**

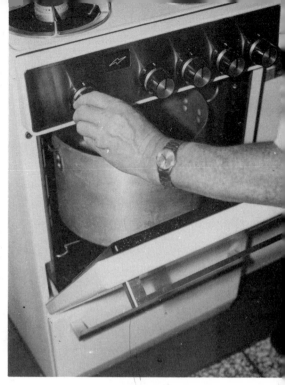

SEPARATION

It is usually recommended that the mash be now transferred to one of the nylon filter bags or 'mash bags' which are available in homebrew shops. The bag should then be placed in or suspended over a vessel with, preferably, a tap at the bottom, the sparge water (at about 170°F) is poured gently and at intervals over the mash and the wort collected through the tap.

I do not consider this attempt to simulate a brewery mash is necessary or effective and it is doubtful that maximum extraction is achieved.

My method is merely to dilute slightly the mash in the jam boiler with some sparge water at 170°F. I then scoop out a bit of mash at a time in a nylon strainer and hold this over a collecting vessel and pour a little of the sparge water through, finally pressing it with something like a cup or basin and continuing until all the mash is finished. The 'squashed' grain may be remixed with a little sparge and put through again to obtain maximum extraction.

17

5. After conversion dilute the mash and pour through strainer into collecting vessel.

6. Put a little more hot water at about 170°F through husks in strainer.

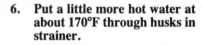

7. Press out last runnings of wort.

8. Cool a sample of the collected wort to check gravity.

9. Check gravity. The optimum gravity of any quantity of wort is about 1045. If higher wort is still left in grain, if lower too much water has been used.

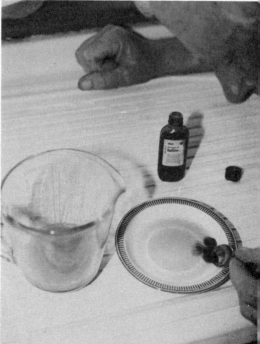

10. Iodine test on wort collected. If reaction is blue, conversion has not been achieved and starch is still present.

11. Transfer collected wort into boiling pan through strainer to remove any husk still remaining. Put spent grain on the roses or feed it to your chickens.

12. Add hops and sugar and boil for about 1½ hours. Gravity will increase as evaporation takes place.

I have had great success with an old spin dryer. After saccharification, the mash is put into a straining bag (or a pair of tights!) and arranged in the spin dryer. The wort is readily collected through the pipe where the washing water is spun out of clothes. I give it three spins, rearranging the bag each time, and use half a gallon of sparge per lb of malt, divided between the three spins.

Whatever method you use, you will now have the malt wort which is the basis of the brew. After adjusting to the required gravity by dilution with water, it is boiled with hops to give an 'all malt' brew. One and a half lbs of good malt fully extracted should yield one gallon of wort at 1.045 gravity.

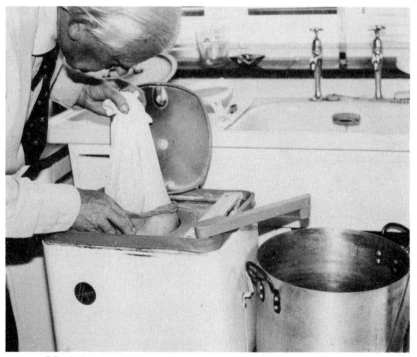

Mash is placed in straining bag and placed in spin dryer.

Above: Sparge water added to mash.

Below: Close lid and spin dryer separates wort from husk completely, giving maximum extract.

CHAPTER 3

Hopping and Boiling

After the malt sugars have been 'sparged' away from the husks in the mash tun they go forward to the essential process of being boiled with hops, the second main ingredient of beer.

The cones or flower of the hop plant *humulus lupulus* are incorporated in beer to give the pleasant bitterness which balances its malt flavour. Before the introduction of hops in the 15th century many herbs such as penny royal, balsam, mint, tansy, sage, dandelion, nettle and even hay had been used but the use of hops quickly spread and became universal. There were the usual outcries by resistant brewers, quacks and parliamentarians who called it a "noxious weed".

Tryon, in his 'A New Art of Brewing' of 1691, said of hops: "There is in them a most excellent glance or friendly opening quality, more especially if they were dried in the sun, for the spirituous parts of this plant is so nice, that it cannot indure any violent heat without prejudice to its fine virtues. Hops naturally purges powerfully by urine so they are unjustly charged to breed the stone, for on the contrary, they are a special remedy against it."

Hops are obviously a useful diuretic! They stimulate the kidneys and also the appetite but it was not their medicinal value or the pleasant flavour they gave to fermented malt liquors which eventually made them invaluable. The resins in hops act as a preservative which protects beer from the subsequent growth of spoilage bacteria, ensuring the soundness and stability of the beer without danger to health or harm to the later addition of yeast to the brew.

Hops also contain a small proportion of tannin which plays a vital part in coagulation and precipitation of malt protein during the boil.

The resins of the hops give colloidal properties to the beer which have a decisive bearing on the foaming and head retention of the finished product.

Analyses of hops vary greatly according to type and seasonal change but the constituents are up to 20% resins, up to 10% pectin, up to 5% tannin, about .5% oil and the remainder physical residue.

The resins subdivide into alpha and beta types which produce *humulon* and *lupulon*. The bitterness comes largely from *humulon* but both contribute antiseptic properties. These substances are not known in any other plant product. The oil contributes to aroma and pectin and tannin in addition to the previously mentioned properties give some astringency in flavour.

Nowadays hops are assessed on their physical appearance and on their E.B.U. number. This stands for European Bitterness Unit and gives a good indication of the general value of the particular hop.

The hop plant was originally just a hedgerow weed in the same general family as the nettle. It is a perennial plant and produces a fresh bine annually which may grow to a length of 25 ft and will climb on any available support. The hop produces male and female flowers on different plants. Pollination is wind blown and is allowed by English hop growers and produces a heavily seeded hop flower or cone.

In Europe, male plants are excluded over a wide area near hop gardens and the result is the seedless Continental hop.

The main hop growing districts in England are Kent, Hampshire and Worcester, with a little overlap into neighbouring counties, but Kent grows more than the total of the other areas and I would consider that about 15,000 tons of hops are grown annually.

Hop growing in the 19th and early 20th century was a highly profitable but highly speculative occupation and, while many growers made fortunes, an equal number went bankrupt.

This was regularised in the 1920s by the setting up of the Hop Marketing Board, which prescribes where and how many hop gardens are used and buys the grower's output. The Board tots up the cost and sells to established merchants, who virtually allocate what the breweries may have and what they have to pay.

This has been satisfactory, but has tended towards hops being

24

grown for decades in the same soil from the same roots, which has led to various pests and diseases attacking them which might have been avoided by fresh plantings in virgin soil, but that is impractical.

A great deal of hybridisation has therefore been done to produce new resistant strains and over the years this has produced new names of hops such as Brewers Gold and Northern Brewer but they are derivatives from the basic English Fuggle and Golding varieties. The Fuggle type is a good strong flavoured general purpose hop for the boil of mild and bitter beers, while the Golding is a more delicately flavoured and aromatic hop for best bitters and pale ales.

Many visitors to Kent will have noticed the 'hop gardens', which are really very large fields with the rows of poles and wirework up which the bines grow each year. By August, the flowers or cones have formed and will have ripened by September, when picking takes place.

The armies of pickers from London no longer arrive: mechanisation has taken over. The bines are cut down completely to ground level and taken to the farm, where they are stripped by machine. The hops are then carefully dried in oast houses by hot air in which a small amount of sulphur is burned, forming sulphur dioxide, as a preservative. The dried hops are pressure packed in large sacks called hop pockets and are kept until required in cold store.

The hops are introduced into the brew when the boiling vessel is being made up from the runnings from the mash and are fully incorporated during the boil.

The sweet wort from the mash tun runs in most breweries to a collecting vessel called an 'underback' and any added sugar would be dissolved in this vessel before flowing on to the boiling vessel.

The boiling vessel is usually of spherical shape, traditionally made of copper and always referred to as "the copper", and still is, although most new vessels are now made of stainless steel.

In early days, the coppers had concave bottoms under which a coal fire provided the heat and many old brewers believe this produced the finest beer because the intense local heat produced more caramelisation and flavour. Nowadays the boil is invariably done by steam heating.

Breweries usually have several different-sized coppers. It will be realised that the first runnings from the mash will be strong, high gravity worts and some of these may be run into a small copper to make up a high gravity beer or barley wine, and the remaining weaker worts divided into coppers for a best bitter and a light bitter.

It will take several hours for mash runnings to make up the copper and during this time the wort temperature is kept up to just under boiling and the hops are gradually fed in to the amount demanded by the type of beer being brewed. A guide to this is given in the following table:

Type of Beer	Gravity	lbs Hops per barrel of beer (36 gallons)
Pale Ale/Bitter	1055	1¾–2¼
Pale Ale/Bitter	1048	1¼–1½
Light Bitter	1040	1–1¼
Mild Ale	1040	⅞–1⅛
Strong Ale	1070	2–3
Stout	1040	1–1½
Stout	1055	1½–2
Lager	1040	½–¾
Lager	1048	1–1¼

The home brewer will be able to work out his hop rates from the above. For example a 1040 bitter requires 1 lb of hops for 36 gallons, therefore one gallon would require 16 ozs divided by 36 which is 0.44 ozs and a five gallon brew would require 2.22, or 2¼ ozs.

It will be noted that the stronger the beer the more hops are required. This is because in the later fermentation a greater bittering loss occurs in the stronger beers.

All that is required from the mash is obtained; the copper is made up to the gallonage and gravity required and the contents are vigorously boiled for about one and half hours. The reasons for boiling are:

1. Evaporation.
2. Sterilisation to knock out bacteria certain to be present in malt and the mash.
3. Killing off enzymes required in malting and mashing but harmful in later fermentation.
4. The full extraction of the hops.
5. As hop resins are extracted, they react with malt protein and help cause the –
6. Flocculation and coagulation of protein.
7. A small amount of caramelisation of wort sugars.

At the completion of the boil, a blending of the bitter substances of the hops and the sweetness extracted from the malt has been achieved and the resins of the hops have assisted in the coagulation of complex proteins. A large diameter valve is opened in the base of the copper to allow a rapid discharge or 'casting' into another vessel called the hop back. A simple vessel with a filter plate bottom to hold back the now spent hops when the hopped wort is pumped away.

In the hop back, the brewer will see that the boil has achieved the 'hot break'. The hops will settle on to the plates and the wort will look black and clear compared with the muddy brown before boiling. The protein coagulation will settle on to the bed of hops and this is a natural filter to hold back hops and protein matter or 'trub' as the clear wort is pumped away, passed through a plate heat exchanger cooler, and on to the fermenting vessel at a temperature of about 60°F, where yeast will be added.

The brewer will have calculated that the beer collected for fermentation will be a few degrees above the required gravity. He then works out the amount of water needed to adjust this and puts the water through the copper, the bed of hops, through the cooler and on to the fermenting vessel. He thus adjusts the gravity and does not lose wort in his plant and piping.

The spent grain left in the mash tun is sold to the farming industry as a cattle feed and spent hops to be incorporated in horticultural fertilisers.

The home brewer will see from this article that boiling of wort from his mash with hops should always be done and this will apply in later articles dealing with brews from extract of malt and hopped kits.

The boiling of malt wort is essential to coagulate protein, and this is the biggest factor in producing clarity in the beer after fermentation.

It is difficult to boil large amounts (five gallons) in the house and I therefore boil the strong section of the wort from the mash (or a dilution of concentrated extract) with the hops and pass this through a fine nylon strainer so that the hop bed filters out the 'hot break' protein. Top up with cold water.

There are alternatives available for the brewer and the homebrewer, to the use of the full cone or flower of the hop in their brewing and these are hop pellets and hop extracts.

These are increasingly being used by commercial brewers and are also available to the homebrewer. Hop pellets are made from 100% hop cones but the 'strig', or skeleton, of the hop flower and the seeds are removed and the leaves or petals of the cone, which bear the resins, tannin and oils, are ground into a powder. These are then pelletised under high pressure and the heat generated by the pressure softens the resin of the hop, which then acts as a natural binder of the pellet.

When boiled in the wort, the pellets disintegrate and give the same contribution to the beer as normal hop cones. However, the brewer will have lost the chance of filtration of malt protein, or 'trub' which is obtained by passing the boiled wort through the bed of spent hops in the 'hop back' vessel and this problem has led to the hop back being replaced by a vessel called the 'Whirlpool'.

In the whirlpool process, the wort is discharged from the copper boil at an angle into a circular vessel and the whirlpool effect causes the trub and hop debris to build up as a mound in the bottom centre of the vessel. The wort is then pumped away for cooling, from an outlet at the side.

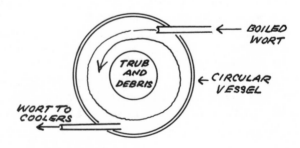

I know some brewers who use pellets and have not introduced a whirlpool, or converted their circular hop backs into whirlpools, but are content to let the fine debris and trub go through to the fermenting vessel where it will settle out with the yeast deposits – and these breweries produce fine beers.

The homebrewer who uses pellets should substitute about 5% less of pellets for the weight of normal hops given in his recipe and after boiling may choose to pass the wort through a fine nylon strainer or let the wort go straight into the fermenting vessel for the debris to settle out there.

The Germans were making hop extract in the middle of the last century, using ethanol as the extracting solvent. At the turn of the century, Great Britain started to manufacture extract of hops, first with ethanol, and later with methanol, as the solvent. By the 1970s methylene chloride was the solvent; in the last few years, the extraction of hops has been most efficiently done by liquid carbon dioxide. With this last method, the low temperature of liquid CO_2 and its inert characteristic ensures extraction without any changes to the resin of the hop and the aroma of the hop is preserved in the extract.

Hop extracts may be used as complete or partial replacement of hops in the copper boil and they are also widely used in the ready hopped concentrates which are the contents of most homebrew beer kits.

A recent development is that of isomerised hop extract. When normal hops are boiled in the malt wort the resins, particularly the alpha acid humolon, are changed into iso-alpha acids, or isohumolone. A similar process is done in the preparation of isomerised hop extract. The result is an extract with all the characteristics of hops boiled in wort and retaining only the bittering substances, which are readily soluble in fermented beer and are now being increasingly used by commercial brewers to adjust bitterness after fermentation.

I can usually detect it in a beer, particularly if heavily used. It is a pleasant bitterness but it is a little different from normal hop palate; however, it might well become the norm. Isomerised hop extract for post fermentation bittering is becoming available to homebrewers and is a very simple way of increasing bitterness if this is thought to be insufficient after fermentation has finished. A very few drops (the exact amount per gallon is usually stated on the label) are dissolved in cooled boiled water and stirred into the beer a day or two before racking off into bottle or keg. Remember isomerised, often called iso extract, is the only hop extract that can also be used *after* fermentation.

I continue to boil fresh hops, much to the consternation of neighbours, who think I am starting a brewery, but there is nothing wrong with modern hop extracts; they are a very useful addition to the armoury of the homebrewer and are very convenient.

CHAPTER 4

Water in Brewing

The water, or "liquor", as brewers call it, used in brewing, is often claimed to be of great importance, but it is my belief that, although treatment is beneficial, this is over-stressed.

We have all heard that the well-known Irish stout is brewed from the waters of a hallowed Irish river, but this is not so and in the same company's London brewery, to the best of my knowledge, they use water straight from the London Metropolitan Water Board! (M.W.B.).

When the hundreds of breweries were established, as Britain became an industrial nation, they invariably sank an artesian well to provide their own water supplies and these waters contained the salts from the strata through which they had filtered. It soon became apparent that certain localities had water naturally suitable for brewing certain types of beer, the most famous of these were Burton upon Trent for bitter beers and pale ales and Edinburgh, for similar beers. London water suited the production of soft flavoured mild beers. On the Continent, Dortmund and Pilsen became famous for lagers.

From the chart showing the main characteristics of several regional brewing waters, it will be seen that the bitter beer and pale ale centres of Burton and Edinburgh both contain high proportions of sulphates, mainly calcium and magnesium, with a little sodium. Dortmund is similar and also has a reputation for pale beers and lagers.

London and Pilsen are ideal soft waters for mild ales, stouts and dark lagers.

All areas except Pilsen show a proportion of carbonates or chalk and this is not beneficial in mashing and fermentation as it makes the brew too alkaline, inhibiting mash reaction and yeast performance.

Salts	Burton-on-Trent		Edinburgh		London (M.W.B.)		Dortmund		Pilsen	
	Parts per 100,000	Grains per gallon	Parts per 100,000	Grains per gallon	Parts per 100,000	Grains per gallon	Parts per 100,000	Grains per gallon	Parts per 100,000	Grains per gallon
Sodium Nitrate $NaNO_3$	4.2	2.9	4.2	2.9	0.4	0.3				
Sodium Chloride $NaCL$	4.7	3.3	10.0	7.0	2.9	2.0	17.5	12.2	0.82	0.57
Sodium Sulphate Na_2SO_4			12.8	9.0	3.6	2.5				
Magnesium Sulphate $MgSO_4$	30.0	21.0	18.0	12.6	1.8	1.3	11.4	8.0	0.42	0.29
Calcium Sulphate $CaSO_4$	59.2	41.4			2.7	1.9	27.2	19.5	0.34	0.24
Calcium Carbonate $CACO_3$	23.5	16.5	35.0	24.5	20.5	14.4	45.0	31.5	1.50	1.05
Sodium Carbonate Na_2CO_3										
Magnesium Carbonate $MgCO_3$										

Brewers in areas not blessed with ideal water introduced water treatment to add or subtract what they wanted and this, basically, involves the removal of carbonates and the introduction of sulphates as required.

The carbonates are usually precipitated out by prolonged boiling and, during this procedure, calcium sulphate (gypsum) is boiled into the solution. However, it is very difficult to get gypsum into solution, while magnesium sulphate goes into solution with water immediately.

Another practice is to change the carbonates chemically into sulphates by adding sulphuric acid to the water and the equation is:

$$CACO_3 + H_2SO_4 = CASO_4 + H_2O + CO_2$$

| Calcium Carbonate | Sulphuric Acid | Calcium Sulphate | Water | CO_2 Gas |

It requires 98 parts by weight of sulphuric acid to neutralise 100 parts by weight of carbonate in the water and change it to sulphate.

This probably gave rise to the fallacy of "chemical brewing", but it is a perfectly natural change in the water and the amount of added acid is minute in the volume of water treated. In fact, it is about 0.008 oz sulphuric acid to one gallon of water, should a homebrewer care to try it when he has a typical chalky water supply.

Brewers do not entirely eliminate carbonates and consider about 10 to 20 grains per gallon acceptable and, some believe, necessary. For pale ales and bitters, sulphates are added to 'Burtonise' the water. These requirements are as follows:

PARTS PER 100,000

	Pale Ale & Bitters Gravity 1.050	Pale Ale & Bitters Gravity 1.040	Mild Ales Gravity 1.040	Stouts Gravity 1.040
Calcium Sulphate	44	27	14	—
Magnesium Sulphate	9	7.5	6	5
Sodium Chloride	4.5	2.5	9	12
Calcium Chloride	4.5	2.0	9	12

Grains per gallon = parts per 100,000 x 0.7

Water treatment is not completely necessary in mashing and fermentation but can give a perceptible improvement in extract, fermentability and flavour – but these are only marginal. Satisfactory brews can be made without treatment.

Most city and regional waters are similar to London M.W.B. and if the homebrewer has a water softener that will eliminate the carbonates (chalk), he will only be concerned with adding sulphates.

The homebrewer will know if he is in a hard water area (chalky) because his kitchen kettle will fur up with a white chalk deposit over a period of months or a year or so.

A wide area of Britain obtaining water from mountain streams feeding reservoirs will have no carbonate problem – these areas will be Manchester and Lancashire (who "steal" their water from my native Wales!) Yorkshire (from the Pennines), certain areas of Scotland and most of South Wales, served by the Brecon Beacons.

The brewer in other areas will have to boil the carbonates out if he does not wish to try a chemical change with acid.

34

It will need a prolonged boil and I would suggest boiling only the amount of water required for mashing and sparging. This will be at least six gallons of water for a five gallon brew, allowing for evaporation, and a vessel such as a jam boiler is required. Bring to the boil and simmer for about six hours.

The sulphates should be added to this boil at the beginning, as calcium sulphate (gypsum) is extremely difficult to get into solution. A half-pint cup can be added to a five gallon brew and by no means all of this will go into solution. Two ounces of magnesium sulphate (Epsom salts) should also be added and this goes into solution immediately; 2 oz of calcium chloride (salt) completes the necessary treatment for bitters and pale ales. A worthwhile addition is a tablespoonful of citric acid to be sure that the acidity of the mash is about pH 5.

With mild ales, the calcium and magnesium sulphates should be cut by half and salt increased to 6 oz. For stouts, calcium should be omitted and 1½ oz only of magnesium sulphate used. Salt can be increased to 9 oz for a sweet stout, but remaining at 6 oz for a normal stout.

These measures are not critical; too little will not be significant and too much will also do no harm to the brew. When I have nothing to hand for water treatment I have often tipped all of a 4 oz tin of Andrews liver salts into my brew. It contains citric acid and magnesium sulphate and the "inner cleanliness" aspect of the salts are adequately lost in five gallons!

The proof!

CHAPTER 5

Weights and Measures

It would be logical now to proceed to fermentation but I believe that, before we discuss this, we should spend a little time on how the brewer works out what weight of materials he uses to obtain the gallonage required, at the strength required.

Breweries are closely controlled by their local Customs and Excise officer. All materials which will yield or dissolve into fermentable solutions must be available for checking by Excise and accurate records kept of intake, use and stock. The Excise authorities supply the brewery with a White Book in which the brewer is required to enter his intention to brew, 24 hours in advance. Not less than 2 hours before starting the brew the brewer has to enter the exact amount of materials he will be using. At the end of the brew the beer made goes to a collecting vessel in which it will ferment. These fermenting or collecting vessels are all gauged by Excise who will mark a dip position on the vessel and supply a dipstick graduated in inches. When the brew is fully collected, the brewer will enter in the White Book, against the relative 'notice', and weights, the dip in inches and the specific gravity of the beer before fermentation starts. The Excise officer therefore will know the exact gallonage and strength of the brew and he also knows what the materials used should yield and, if they do not tally, very awkward questions will be asked of the brewer! The Excise duty is levied on the strength or specific gravity before fermentation (original gravity) and gallonage and, at the end of each month, the brewer will receive a duty bill for all beers collected in that month, which must be promptly paid.

A major part of the cost of beer sold to the public is duty paid on strength and, in my opinion, it is unsatisfactory that some sort of indication of strength and therefore, duty paid, is not stated on beer. The omission allows some low gravity beers, with fancy names, to sell at a higher price than 'value-for-money' beers of a higher gravity. Discussions are going on with E.E.C. to introduce gravity bands, which should give some validity to the price asked.

The brewer must know how much fermentable material he has to use to obtain the required gallonage of beer at the required strength and discussing this should help those home brewers who like to make up their own brews. The first thing to be considered is specific gravity.

This is simply the ratio between the mass of a substance occupying a given volume and water in the same volume and is measured as density compared with water.

We have washed malt sugars from the mash and this has made the fermentable wort denser than water. The more dense the solution in the wort, the stronger will be the final beer. With water as 1.000, a comparative scale of densities has been worked out and, to avoid fractions and decimals, this is multiplied by 1000. A medium strength wort, for example would be 1045, against the 1000 of water.

The simple instrument, the hydrometer, which brewers call a saccharometer, is used to determine this gravity. It is merely a glass float weighted at the bottom and extended from the top into a stem. The stem shows a graduated scale, which covers the normal beer range of gravities (usually marked from 1000 to 1100), subdivided into tens, with the tens subdivided into single degrees. The hydrometer is floated in the wort to be tested. In water it will sink to the 1000 mark but in a denser wort, with malt or other sugars in solution, it floats higher.

A reading is taken where the liquid line intersects the scale, let us say, at 42. This, in fact, is 1042 or 1.042 if the x1000 is not used.

The graduations might vary in the scale markings of some makers and, with different flotation and weighting, hydrometers can be made for different ranges of specific gravities. Whatever the type, it is a simple way of showing density compared with water. For greatest accuracy, all readings must be taken at 60°F.

Customs and Excise use specific gravity to decide taxation on the original gravity before fermentation. The brewer uses specific gravity, to show his original gravity having decided the strength of his beer. Let us say that a brewer intends to brew 500 barrels (a barrel = 36 gallons) at 1045 gravity. How does he work out his requirements of malt and any adjuncts to brew this amount accurately? Here we must use more brewing terms and these are "brewers' pounds per barrel;" the "extract value" of materials are linked to this.

Before specific gravity was adopted, brewers used brewers' lbs, or saccharometer lbs, per barrel as their yardstick and as the expected yield, or extract, of malt, sugars and adjuncts is always given in brewers' lbs it is still used. The term 'brewers lbs' merely means the weight of a barrel (36 gallons) of water compared with a barrel of wort with malt and other sugars in solution.

This can be related to specific gravity and this is shown in the tables overleaf.

All materials used in brewing which yield fermentable sugars have an extract value stated as brewers' lbs (brs lbs) per barrel for a given amount. The main fermentable yielder is malt (as grain). This is variable owing to differences in malt quality but may be assumed to be 90–100 brs lbs per quarter (336 lbs).

At this stage we are only considering an 'all malt' and hops beer and will discuss various adjuncts later. They all have an extract value which I will give when describing them. Most sugars, for example, have a value of 72 brs. lbs per 224 lbs.

Hops, of course, do not give any gravity or fermentable matter and only contribute flavour and antiseptic value to the brew plus colloidal foam and "head" forming properties.

Let us return to our brewer, who is going to brew 500 barrels of 1045 gravity beer. Referring to the table shown he will find that 1045 specific gravity is 16.2 brs lbs per barrel and he will therefore require 500 x 16.2 brs lbs which is 8100 brs lbs.

His tests have shown that the malt in use is giving a lab. extract of 95 brs lbs per quarter (336 lbs) and he will therefore require 85.26 quarters (8100 ÷ 95) of malt or 28,647.36 lbs. He will add about 2% to this figure to counteract losses in plant and adsorbtion by hops in boiling and he will convert back his final 29,220 lbs into tons or hundred weights, quarters or metric measures whichever he may be using for bulk figures in the brewery.

It would be advisable to use 1¼ lbs of hops per barrel in this brew and therefore 625 lbs of hops would be boiled with the wort obtained from the malt.

39

BREWERS' POUNDS, S.G. 1000.55 – 1105

Lb. per barrel	Specific gravity	Lb. per barrel	Specific gravity	Lb. per barrel	Specific gravity
0		8	1022.22	16	1044.44
.2	1000.55	.2	1022.77	.2	1045.00
.4	1001.11	.4	1023.33	.4	1045.55
.6	1001.66	.6	1023.88	.6	1046.11
.8	1002.22	.8	1024.44	.8	1046.66
1	1002.77	9	1025.00	17	1047.22
.2	1003.33	.2	1025.55	.2	1047.77
.4	1003.88	.4	1026.11	.4	1048.33
.6	1004.44	.6	1026.66	.6	1048.88
.8	1005.00	.8	1027.22	.8	1049.44
2	1005.55	10	1027.77	18	1050.00
.2	1006.11	.2	1028.33	.2	1050.55
.4	1006.66	.4	1028.88	.4	1051.11
.6	1007.22	.6	1029.44	.6	1051.66
.8	1007.77	.8	1030.00	.8	1052.22
3	1008.33	11	1030.55	19	1052.77
.2	1008.88	.2	1031.11	.2	1053.33
.4	1009.44	.4	1031.66	.4	1053.88
.6	1010.00	.6	1032.22	.6	1054.44
.8	1010.55	.8	1032.77	.8	1055.00
4	1011.11	12	1033.33	20	1055.55
.2	1011.66	.2	1033.88	.2	1056.11
.4	1012.22	.4	1034.44	.4	1056.66
.6	1012.77	.6	1035.00	.6	1057.22
.8	1013.33	.8	1035.55	.8	1057.77
5	1013.88	13	1036.11	21	1058.33
.2	1014.44	.2	1036.66	.2	1058.88
.4	1015.00	.4	1037.22	.4	1059.44
.6	1015.55	.6	1037.77	.6	1060.00
.8	1016.11	.8	1038.33	.8	1060.55
6	1016.66	14	1038.88	22	1061.11
.2	1017.22	.2	1039.44	.2	1061.66
.4	1017.77	.6	1040.00	.4	1062.22
.6	1018.33	.6	1040.55	.6	1062.77
.8	1018.88	.8	1041.11	.8	1063.33
7	1019.44	15	1041.66	23	1063.88
.2	1020.00	.2	1042.22	.2	1064.44
.4	1020.55	.4	1042.77	.4	1065.00
.6	1021.11	.6	1043.33	.6	1065.55
.8	1021.66	.8	1043.88	.8	1066.11

40

BREWERS' POUNDS, S.G. 1000.55 – 1105

Lb. per barrel	Specific gravity	Lb. per barrel	Specific gravity	Lb. per barrel	Specific gravity
24	1066.66	31	1086.11	38	1105.55
.2	1067.22	.2	1086.66	.2	1106.11
.4	1067.77	.4	1087.22	.4	1106.66
.6	1068.33	.6	1087.77	.6	1107.22
.8	1068.88	.8	1088.33	.8	1107.77
25	1069.44	32	1088.88	39	1108.33
.2	1070.00	.2	1089.44	.2	1108.88
.4	1070.55	.4	1090.00	.4	1109.44
.6	1071.11	.6	1090.55	.6	1110.00
.8	1071.66	.8	1091.11	.8	1110.55
26	1072.22	33	1091.66	40	1111.11
.2	1072.77	.2	1092.22	.2	1111.66
.4	1073.33	.4	1092.77	.4	1112.22
.6	1073.88	.6	1093.33	.6	1112.77
.8	1074.44	.8	1093.88	.8	1113.33
27	1075.00	34	1094.44	41	1113.88
.2	1075.55	.2	1095.00	.2	1114.44
.4	1076.11	.4	1095.55	.4	1115.00
.6	1076.66	.6	1096.11	.6	1115.55
.8	1077.22	.8	1096.66	.8	1116.11
28	1077.77	35	1097.22	42	1116.66
.2	1078.33	.2	1097.77	.2	1117.22
.4	1078.88	.4	1098.33	.4	1117.77
.6	1079.44	.6	1098.88	.6	1118.33
.8	1080.00	.8	1099.44	.8	1118.88
29	1080.55	36	1100.00	43	1119.44
.2	1081.11	.2	1100.55	.2	1120.00
.4	1081.66	.4	1101.11	.4	1120.55
.6	1082.22	.6	1101.66	.6	1121.11
.8	1082.77	.8	1102.22	.8	1121.66
30	1083.33	37	1102.77	44	1122.22
.2	1083.88	.2	1103.33	.2	1122.77
.4	1084.44	.4	1103.88	.4	1123.33
.6	1085.00	.6	1104.44	.6	1123.88
.8	1085.55	.8	1105.00	.8	1124.44
				45	1125.00

41

A PREMIUM ALL MALT HOME BREW

ALL MALT PALE ALE

To make 5 galls (450 g).
8 lbs pale malt
2½ oz Golding hops

From these figures we can work out a premium all malt mashed brew of five gallons at 1045 gravity. We will assume that we have a good pale ale malt of 95 extract. 1045 gravity is 16.2 brs lbs per barrel of 36 gallons. We only want 5 gallons and therefore require 2.25 brs lbs (5 x 16.2 ÷ 36). Our malt gives 95 brs lbs per 336 lbs and we will want 7.95 lbs for our 5 gallons (2.25 x 336 ÷ 95). Round this up to 8 lbs.

The malt may be purchased ready ground as grist or whole. If whole, roughly crush in a coffee mill or roll or hammer the corns on a hard, flat surface.

Mash in 2 gallons of water at 165°F to obtain a mash heat of 150°F. Hold heat and stand for about two hours. Sparge and filter as suggested in Chapter 2 with 2 gallons of water at 170°F.

Boil the wort obtained in a large vessel, with 2½ ozs Golding hops, for one and a half hours. Hops should be free in the boil and *not* in a muslin bag as often suggested.

After the boil, pass the wort through a nylon strainer to remove the now spent hops. I collect in a separate vessel but the wort can go straight into the fermenting vessel. It is advisable to have about 10 pints of cold water in the fermenting vessel to receive the hot wort. Top up to 5 gallons. I find it best to leave a 5 gallon mark and as this is approached stir vigorously to mix wort and water. Take a hydrometer reading. This enables you to check whether you have achieved a good extraction from the mash. If you have not you will have to decide either, to stop short of 5 gallons to obtain the 1045 gravity or settle for 5 gallons at a lower gravity.

Ferment with a sachet of dried yeast or, if you are lucky, a cupful of yeast from a cooperative local brewery. This brew will ferment to a stop position of about 1008–1010 depending on yeast used and should then be bottled or kegged with a little priming (a half teaspoon per bottle or 2½–03 per five gallon keg) and fining.

Typical brewery yeast, showing budding cells, magnified 1000 times.

CHAPTER 6

Yeast and Fermentation

As the fermenting vessel is filling the brewer will add his strain of yeast to the wort and fermentation will begin.

What is fermentation? Although beers and wines had been fermented for over 1000 years and the brewers knew that the creamy sludge that formed in the fermenting liquid was the cause, they were ignorant of what took place. They did know that it was necessary to collect this yeasty sludge from one brew to reintroduce it to the next.

In 1837, W. H. Roberts wrote "Discussion of the subject of fermentation would be of little real benefit to the operator; for confidently as many have asserted their knowledge of its secret causes and effects, the mystery in which its principles are involved continues to present an unpenetrated barrier; those who dogmatically profess to have encompassed this subtle and complicated subject only prove the extent of their ignorance and presumption".

In fact, at the beginning of the 19th Century there was fierce dispute between two schools of thought on fermentation. One side claimed that yeast was a vegetable plant which caused the change of fermentable sugars to an alcoholic drink and the other, led by famous chemists like Liebig and Lavoisier, held that fermentation was merely a chemical action.

A whole host of researchers too numerous to mention have left records of their work, but it was not until 1857 that the truth was established. Louis Pasteur was investigating the killing disease of Anthrax, passed from sheep's wool to humans and causing malignant pustules to break out. He thought some organism was being transmitted. He therefore studied fermentation in wine and his "Études sur le Vin" (studies on wine) and later, in 1876, "Études sur la Bière" (studies on beer) established that yeast was a microscopic single cell living organism which fed on and multiplied in any suitable fermentable sugar solution. Lavoisier and others capitulated.

Significant was an earlier discovery, in 1830, by Dubrunfaut, that an extract of malt converted starch to sugar by what he called diastase, but which was not yet recognised as an enzyme. In 1897, Buchner found the final link between Pasteur and the chemical change by discovering that the living cells of yeast depended on enzymes generated by themselves for their own life and these enzymes caused the conversion of sugars to alcohol and carbon dioxide gas in the fermentation process.

All this work led to a fundamental change, not only in brewing and winemaking, but in the whole field of medicine, where it was eventually accepted that disease was invariably caused by organisms or bacteria. This knowledge led to anti-sepsis and sterilising by "Pasteurisation" and, later, the fermentation-produced antibiotics, which are yeast or mould type organisms whose enzymes combat those of bacterial illness. We take all this for granted today and everyone washes, gargles antiseptics, cleans their teeth, puts wonder liquid that "kills all known germs" in the sink and to "go round the bend" – but before Pasteur, all this was a complete blank.

A new light came into brewing when it was realised that yeast was a living organism and with the succeeding knowledge of the bacterial infection and spoiling of beer and other products by wild yeasts and other organisms.

As early as 1883, Emil Hansen in the Danish Carlsberg brewery had found that brewery yeasts were a mixture of the thousands of species in existence and that wild yeasts and various bacteria caused defects in his beer. He therefore selected a single strain and, in sterile vessels, cultured this in equally sterile wort solution until the multiplication of the yeast gave him sufficient for a large-scale brew.

Brewers will expect yeast to multiply by ten times in any normal fermentation. This multiplying is caused by individual cells 'budding'. Under the microscope, cells can be seen to develop a bulge which grows and becomes rounded like the parent cell and eventually separates to live on its own.

Yeast nowadays is classed in the genus 'Myces' which are about half way between a bacteria and a mould. Beer yeasts are classified as 'Saccharomyces' and there are many strains but, by and large, British beer yeasts are Saccharomyces Cerevisae and on the continent (and in the new British lager breweries) derivatives of Carlsbergensis are used. The broad division between the two is that British beer yeast is top fermenting and the lager yeast ferments mainly from the bottom and at a lower temperature. We are only discussing British beer yeasts and these again can be broadly subdivided into flocculating and non-flocculating. Both flocculate but one flocculates more readily than the other.

Pasteur originally described the action of yeast as "life without air" but this is not strictly correct. Yeast does need some oxygen at the beginning of fermentation, but will continue in an anaerobic state. There is sufficient air in the wort from the boiling, cooling and collecting in the fermenting vessel and the homebrewer should realise this and keep further air away once he has added yeast.

In the brewery, the fermentation is now another controlled engineering operation. The beer ferments, a great deal of surplus yeast is produced, and this has to be separated out of the beer before the beer goes on to be conditioned and put in cask, bottle or keg.

The amount of yeast added to a fermentation is:

Gravity of wort	lbs of thick, liquid yeast per barrel of 36 gallons
1040	¾
1050	1¼
1060	2–2½
1080	2½–3

The homebrewer who can only obtain dried yeast should halve these quantities. Yeast is added at a temperature of 65°F.

There are several methods of fermenting in British breweries and these are:

The Burton Union System.
The Yorkshire Stone Square.
The Skimming System.
The Conical Fermenter.

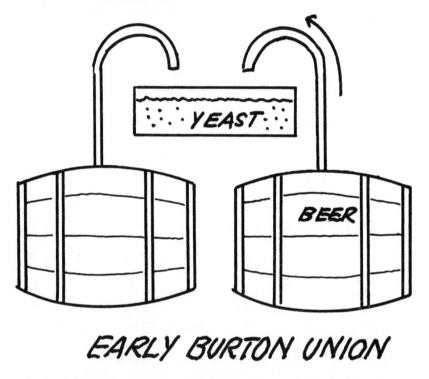

EARLY BURTON UNION

In the **Burton system,** large casks were filled with yeasted wort and a swan neck pipe at the top let into a yeast collecting vessel. The pressure of gas created and the increased volume of yeast simply drove the yeast up and into the collecting vessel. This method is still used but in modern stainless steel form.

The **Yorkshire system** was a slate vessel with a dividing floor at beer level and a funnel in this floor passed yeast into the top

46

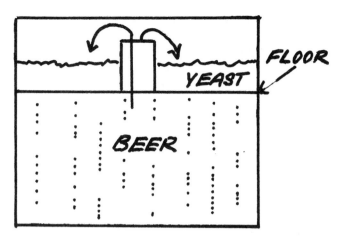

YORKSHIRE STONE SQUARE

compartment. Modern stainless versions of this method continue to be built.

The **Skimming system** is universally used all over Britain and is an open vessel with a funnel-shaped 'parachute', which is lowered to just above beer level and the yeast head is skimmed to the funnel and falls to a collecting vessel beneath.

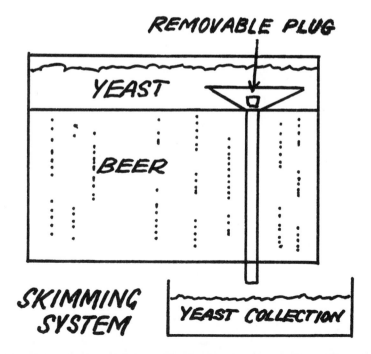

SKIMMING SYSTEM

47

In breweries that have been built in the last 20 years, the **Conical fermenter** is invariably used. It is by no means new and was developed by Nathan, for use in the Nathan system of brewing lager in Australia in the 1930s. It consists of a tall closed round vessel with a cone shaped base. There is a variable pressure relief valve at the top and refrigeration pipes are built into the walls of the vessel, the whole vessel is covered with insulation material. They are usually weatherproofed and they can be seen standing in the open at most of the new breweries.

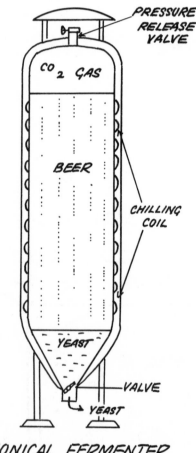

CONICAL FERMENTER

When the fermentation has finished, the beer is chilled down to about 50°F. This causes the yeast to flocculate to the cone at the base and, when opened, the yeast comes out like toothpaste from a tube, to be collected.

All the systems have some method of temperature control, usually cold water pipes arranged as coils in the vessel.

The breweries produce a huge surplus of yeast; it is of high protein value and is used in various foods, animal foods and tonics. When boiled down and concentrated, it makes the well-known black spread in most homes and while there is some beef extract in beef cubes and flavourings the largest ingredient is concentrated yeast.

A properly formulated and brewed beer does not ferment to zero gravity. This is the common fault of homebrewed beers, where too great a proportion of household sugar is used and when the brew has not been boiled. Beer is brewed from malt not sugar and the maltose and glucose extracted from the malt mash will yield all the alcohol, flavour and strength required.

Beer ferments to an end point of about 1/5th to 1/6th of original gravity before fermentation. A graph of a typical fermentation is shown:

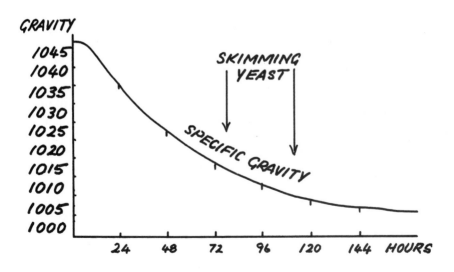

It will be seen that a steep fall in gravity occurs in the first 48 hours and this is due to the oxygen in the wort in the initial stage and also the high proportion of sugars available. It is interesting to note that in the commercial production of yeast for bread, yeast is propagated on molasses, with a constant injection of air. This produces the maximum crop but brewers and homebrewers should exclude air as in the conical fermenter.

FLOCCULATION

Yeasts vary in their habit of flocculation. The Yorkshire and Burton systems require a yeast that flocculates to the top but a large amount of any yeasts go to the bottom and continue fermentation there.

In the skimming system, yeast is often roused back into the beer, as fermentation will stop unless yeast is kept in suspension in the wort, but other types flocculate so slowly that rousing is not necessary.

The creamy balm yeast collected from brewery fermentations is put under pressure through a filter press; beer is squeezed out and returned to the fermenting vessel. The yeast is now of a fairly firm cheesy consistency, some to be kept in a refrigerator for following brews and the surplus sold for the uses previously mentioned.

POINTS FOR HOME BREWERS

The general principles outlined will occur in home brewing, but the choice of yeast available is limited.

The dried yeast in various beer kits and sold in sachets comes, in the main, from one or two commercial yeast propagation plants. Although dried down to small granules it is still a living organism of cell life and becomes active and multiplies in a sweet nutrient. They are not true beer yeasts but any yeast is a 'workhorse' and they are perfectly adequate fermenters of beer. Characteristically, they make an initial head which goes back into the beer and fermentation continues from the bottom. This leaves uncovered beer which is highly susceptible to airborne infection, particularly when initial gassing has finished. The fermenting vessel should be covered at all times.

There is no need for 'starter bottles' or yeast nutrients. A properly prepared malt wort is itself the perfect yeast nutrient. Scatter the granules on top of the wort and put the lid on. You might be lucky enough to obtain yeast from your local brewery and this will be flocculating. Dissolve it in some of your brew and mix in. It will give a large crop on top of the beer; this requires to be roused back into the beer and, later, will need skimming at about S.G. 1010–1015. It then will make a shallow protective cover of yeast on the brew. A 1045 beer made from malt will ferment to an end point of about 1008. Keep covered and let it settle for a day or so, preferably in a cold position, to assist the sedimentation of yeast before bottling or kegging.

There are many good fermenting vessels obtainable, but ideally they should have snap-on lids, a fermentation lock in the lid and a tap about 1″ from the bottom for taking samples and for easy racking off to bottle or keg.

Cleanliness and sterility goes without saying but remember that air is the biggest hazard to small scale fermentation. Temperature should be maintained between 65°F and 75°F.

I use a local brewery yeast. This gives tremendous reproduction and has forced me to use a modified Burton Union system by fitting a tube to the lid of my fermenter, leading to a smaller vessel, which takes the surplus yeast.

MY METHOD

After fermentation we at last have beer in a rough state. Later I will discuss what the brewer does to bring it to the public clear and in good condition and how the homebrewer will achieve this.

Above: Yeast being roused at Boddingtons Brewery, Manchester. Fermenting room is sterile, air conditioned.

Below: Duty brewer checks fermentations.

Conical fermenters at the Courage Berkshire Brewery.

Above: First 'cauliflower' head on my beer using fresh brewers yeast.

Below: Crop of yeast beginning to form.

Below: At 1010 gravity (O.G. 1045) skimming yeast crop into a sterilised jar for storage in refrigerator for next brew.

CHAPTER 7

It's <u>All</u> Real Ale

Brewing is a process of extraction. Sugars are extracted from malted barley and the spent grain or husks are sold as a by-product. Tannins, preservatives and flavour are extracted from the hops and spent hops are sold to be incorporated in horticultural fertilisers. Yeast has fermented the brew and produced a surplus, which is sold to various food outlets.

The beer now in the fermenting vessel is in a fairly rough state. Fermentation has finished at a small residual gravity (1/5th to 1/6th of original gravity) and the beer will be cloudy because there will still be some inactive yeast in suspension – also a certain amount of protein and debris from the extraction process. The beer therefore has to be clarified and conditioned before drinking.

After fermentation the rough beer can now take two distinct routes to the customer. The first of these is by natural conditioning and the acceleration of the clearing process, by the addition of "finings". Conditioning (foam and sparkle) is achieved by adding a small amount of sugar. The result will be the so called real ale, conditioned in cask.

The same beer could take the second route, which involves bulk conditioning in a closed vessel (this is not always required), chilling, sterilising, filtration, adjusting the gas content by injection of CO_2 gas (usually collected from their own fermentations) and probably pasteurisation. Kegs are filled under pressure and dispensed under pressure to the customer. The result is a stabilised, "packaged" article which requires no attention, keeps indefinitely and can be sent anywhere and exported. Also from the second route, beers can be filled into bottles, cans and other containers.

I am a life long devotee of naturally conditioned draught ale but I consider CAMRA (Campaign for the Maintenance of Real Ale) to be presumptuous in fostering the legend that only draught ale is real ale and, therefore, that all other stabilised and keg beers are "un-real" ale.

More rabid members of CAMRA even refer to them as "chemical beers". This, of course, is nonsense; brewers are closely controlled to permitted natural ingredients in beer, and these are brewed and fermented in a completely natural way, even though the size and scale of modern breweries make it appear to be an engineering process.

In scores of breweries, the brew, after fermentation, is split into a proportion for natural conditioning and sold as draught ale and the other portion is stabilised and kegged and they often carry different names.

However, my local brewery brews an excellent "Best Bitter" – in my local it is on draught through a hand pump and in my golf club, still called "Best Bitter", it is in keg. Both are worth drinking and the only difference is the method of preparing it for sale.

There might be some inventive homebrewers with a bent for engineering, who might try stabilising their fermented beer and kegging it. They would have to chill their beer to promote a "chill haze" then filter it. Brewers do this, because once the haze forming proteins are filtered out the beer can later be kept in the cold without "chill haze" reappearing.

After filtration, the beer would be flat and therefore CO_2 gas would have to be injected into it, as no yeast remains to give a secondary fermentation for conditioning. However, just putting the filtered beer into a keg and injecting gas above it will not do. The beer would have to be pumped from the bottom to the top of the keg in a closed circuit and CO_2 gas injected into the beer in the pipe as it passed through. The beer would have to be at 40–50°F to allow gas to go into solution.

This process is not impossible to a good handyman, but there is no real advantage and the homebrewer will find that natural conditioning in bottle or keg gives all that is required.

Let us return to the brewery with fermented beer in the fermenting vessel. The brewer would retain the beer in this vessel for two to three days, to start settling out. It will be protected from the air by its final close head of yeast (homebrew yeasts do not usually have this so the homebrewer must keep his vessel covered). The beer will then be let down into a settling vessel or into a racking tank and from either of these he will fill the casks, which are nowadays mainly metal. Some draught ale buffs pine for beer from the wood but on all counts true draught ale is better from a metal cask. The brewer would like to keep the filled casks cellared for about a week for further settling and maturation. Before delivery to the pub, the cask is opened and a small amount of sugar solution and some finings are added.

In the pub, the landlord will put the cask in its final position. The sugar solution will give a small secondary fermentation with the yeast cells still remaining in the beer and this gives some gas and condition to the beer. The finings will accelerate the clarification of the beer.

Finings are invariably obtained from collagen, which is a protein in fibrous connective animal tissue. Gelatine is boiled out of the gristle and sinews of animal waste and is a useful fining. Beer finings, however, are usually **isinglass,** which is gelatine obtained from the air bladders of Malay Sea sturgeons. The local fishermen remove the bladders and dry them in the sun and they reach European markets as hard, flat, but uneven sheets of semi-transparent isinglass "leaf".

The finings manufacturers steep the isinglass in tartaric acid, plus about 5% sulphurous acid (as a preservative) for some weeks. The "glass" will soften and swell and is then rubbed through sieves until it is completely liquidised. The finings solution is now a glutinous, grey white liquid resembling Gloy office paper adhesive. It is sent in casks to the breweries and is ready to add to the beer.

The brewery will add about one quart of finings to a 36 gallon barrel of beer (also about a quart of sugar solution) just before delivery to the customer.

The colloidal protein of the finings will disperse throughout the beer and the positive and negative electric changes of the various haze solids are neutralized. These, no longer repelling each other, can coagulate and precipitate.

More recent research, with the enormous magnification of the electron microscope, shows that the molecules of collagens such as isinglass resemble thistle burrs; this points to the action being mainly physical, with the burrs collecting the haze formers until they become weighted enough to settle as a deposit.

Finings accelerate the clearing and give a bright "polish" to the beer, which otherwise could only be achieved with time.

All the foregoing points will be applicable to the homebrewer, as he depends on natural conditioning and clearing of his beer in bottles or the various available plastic containers for draught cask beer.

A sterile beer in a sterile container is the aim and this should be achieved with a boiled brew and exclusion of contaminating air at all times. Bottles and plastic kegs must be gas tight to retain the gas made by the addition of priming sugar for conditioning.

A half teaspoonful of sugar per pint should be added at bottling. I prefer to dissolve this in a very small amount of boiling water and add as a syrup to the empty bottle. The advantage of a tap in the fermenting vessel (mentioned in Chapter 6) is now apparent and I also recommend a small length of plastic tubing, to be fitted on the tap – this goes to the bottom of the bottle and allows filling without fobbing or coming into contact with air. Leave a small space at the top of the bottle and cap securely. A small teaspoonful of ready-to-use finings may be added, to ensure brightness.

Keep bottles in a warmish area for a day or two to allow sugar to ferment, then store in a cool position. Do not be afraid of the remaining gravity of a properly made brew. This is a "stop" position and only the added sugar will ferment.

I prefer to put my beer in a five gallon plastic keg and a 1.045 gravity beer fermented to a stop position of 1.008 with five ounces of sugar added in the keg will generate sufficient secondary condition and pressure to dispense the whole five gallons. Protected by the gas made, this will last for months and a pint or so is enjoyed as required. It is essential that the keg is gas-tight and taps and caps must be really firmly tightened up. There are many good casks available now, but I have a preference for an opaque colour so that I can see the amount of beer remaining. I also consider that a float "take off" (which I introduced to home-brewing) is essential. Beer clears from top to bottom and the float allows clear beer to be drawn in a day or two; without one, you could be waiting for weeks for the beer to become clear at tap level.

Your keg should also have a CO_2 valve (incorporating a safety valve to guard against excess pressure) so that gas pressure can be be used if natural pressure fails. You would otherwise have to admit air to allow pouring and then the beer's life would be days only.

Before transferring my beer to a clean and sterile keg, I do fill the keg with CO_2 gas and then, with the plastic tube from my fermenting vessel tap leading to the bottom of the keg, the beer is transferred, without fobbing or having to force its way through the cushion of gas and with no air contact to infect the beer. During filling, the five to six ounces of sugar, as a boiling syrup in a little water, is added, with about an eggcupful of ready-to-use isinglass finings. In two or three days I am enjoying a creamy-headed, malt and hops, best quality bitter and will be doing so until the last pint.

We have now gone through the brewing process from barley to the end product but have dealt only with a straight, malt-only best bitter. In the next chapter I will discuss alternative materials and adjuncts and the quite slight changes in composition required to make different types of beer.

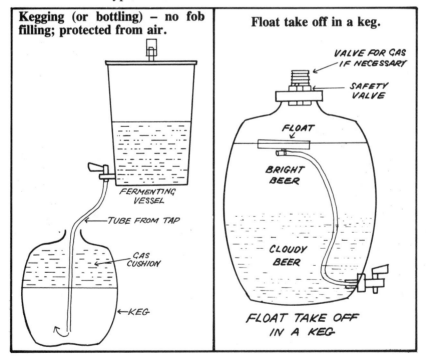

Kegging (or bottling) – no fob filling; protected from air.

FERMENTING VESSEL
TUBE FROM TAP
GAS CUSHION
KEG

Float take off in a keg.

VALVE FOR GAS IF NECESSARY
SAFETY VALVE
FLOAT
BRIGHT BEER
CLOUDY BEER
FLOAT TAKE OFF IN A KEG

Above: Filling empty keg with CO_2 gas to eliminate air.

Below: Adding finings.

Above: Transferring fermented beer to gas filled keg. Priming and fining solutions ready to be added during filling.

Below: Tighten only until you feel the rubber grommet being squeezed.

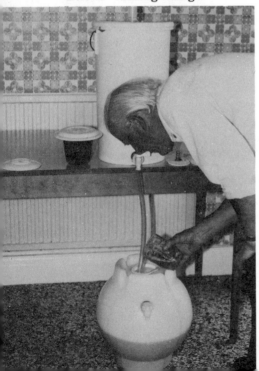

My simple brew house

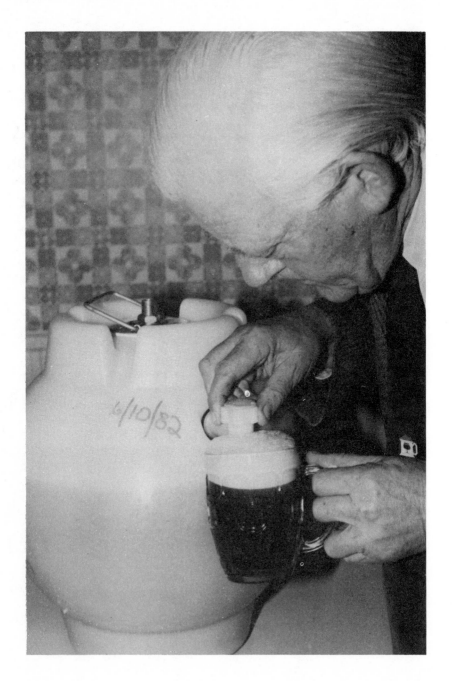

CHAPTER 8

Alternatives and Adjuncts

We have now followed a typical malted barley (malt) and hops only brew from the barley fields and hop gardens to a finished brew in its various containers, draught, keg or bottle. Our example has been a fairly high gravity (1045) beer with a good hop rate of 1½ lb per barrel of 36 gallons.

In the home brew version (Chapter 5) 8 lb of grain malt with 2½ oz of hops were used to produce 5 gallons of 1045 beer. At this hop rate and gravity it is a premium best bitter and it is only really necessary to use malt and hops to produce the best beers in the world.

The changes required to brew different types are very small. A higher coloured malt with less hops and a lower gravity will give a dark mild beer. Less hops and a lower gravity is light ale, roast barley or black malt added produces stout or porter, very lightly cured pale malt and German hops give lager and if half the amount of water is used in our 8 lb premium home brew a double strength barley wine results. It would be advisable to increase the hops by ¼ to ½ oz, not to lose bittering in this stronger fermentation.

So why use adjuncts at all? There really is no need and there is no doubt that many found their way into commercial brewing simply to cut production costs. It was not a question of improving the beer but of "how much can we use without our customers noticing?" This might be a hard judgement but it is a fact that the majority of adjuncts were introduced because they were "cheaper than malt" in producing a portion of the fermentable ingredient of the brew. Some, like sugar, speed up the fermentation and help in the quicker clearing of the beer but time will do this equally well and will not thin out flavour. It can be said that some adjuncts have an effect on flavour but I still feel this is a justification rather than the original reason for using them.

The homebrewer has always been eager to find out what the commercial brewers are using and when he finds big brother is using flaked maize, flaked barley, wheat flour or other unmalted cereals in his mash, he feels he must also do so to achieve the commercial taste. He will also find that sugar, originally used because it was cheaper than malt, has now become more expensive, so the brewer has changed to glucose which is cheaper than sugar and malt.

The homebrewer should be aiming to produce a better beer than the commercial variety and therefore should not slavishly use cheap alternatives to malt. I will describe the above and others, and method of use and their effects, later but now I will deal with an alternative to those homebrewers who do not wish to go through the interesting but time-consuming business of mashing and extracting their wort from grain malt; of course, I refer to malt extract.

MALT EXTRACT

The brown sticky syrup, concentrated extract of malt, is the real reason for, and has made possible the huge interest and growth in homebrewing. It would never have taken off if homebrewers were restricted to mashing and extracting from grain malt, yet the mashers still decry malt extract brews and still speak of the malt extract tang in beers! I totally disagree with this and, although a commercial brewer myself, invariably make up my home brews with malt extract. The legend of the tang persists from early recipes and methods when more sugar than malt extract was used, the brew was not boiled and consequently, fermented to zero gravity or lower, leaving no flavour other than a decided tang from the foul hops then available.

When a large proportion of good malt extract and a very small proportion of sugar (if you must use it) is dissolved and vigorously boiled with good hops and fermented with fresh brewer's yeast a beer of really first class quality is produced. Unfortunately, old recipes and methods are still in print and some beer kits contain only a small amount of malt extract and rely on sugar and a low gravity of beer to obtain the stated number of pints or gallons.

No malt extract is stronger or more concentrated than others. They are all within a point or so of 80% solids.

There is really no reason why malt extract should not produce good beer because an extract factory is exactly like a brewery. Malted barley is taken in, ground and mashed into a brewery mash tun and, after conversion, the sweet wort is collected but, instead of going on to be fermented, is boiled under vacuum until it is concentrated to the 80% solids thick malt syrup.

Why under vacuum? This allows boiling and concentration to occur at very low temperatures and therefore malt enzymes are preserved and no burning or caramelisation takes place. By altering the curing of the malt and mashing and concentration temperatures, a range of extracts is produced with high or low enzyme content, light and dark colour and variable flavours.

For homebrew, typical brewing worts are concentrated. Malt extract may be further dried under vacuum to a dry state and this is also an acceptable main ingredient of a homebrew.

The mashers always quote, "condensed milk and dried milk are not like real milk", but the answer is that they did not start as real milk – condensed milk is sweetened skim milk and dried milk is skim milk only. Malt extract is made from 100% malt and nothing else and when diluted is identical with wort from the mash tun, brews and ferments in the same way and can be used in all recipes as a complete replacement for mash wort.

The extract figure of malt extract, for those brewers who formulate their own brews, is 70 Brewers lbs per 224 lb.

Manufacturers also incorporate hops in the wort before concentration. Hopped malt extract is widely available and is the main ingredient of homebrew kits.

I have to consider sugar, as it is useful as a minor ingredient of beer. It is a pure carbohydrate, $C_{12}H_{22}O_{11}$, extracted from cane or beet, but has no protein and supplies no nutrient to yeast. The yeast will ferment sugar, but will not multiply. It is freely fermentable and ferments right out to zero gravity; it therefore provides no taste to the beer and tends to "dry" the flavour. Never include sugar to make fermentations sweeter, as the reverse is the case.

When a small proportion of sugar is incorporated in the brew, the fermentation will be slightly quicker and the final gravity will be slightly lower than a 100% malt brew. The sugar also dilutes some of the nitrogenous protein of the malt and leads to quicker clearing of the beer. In commercial brewing, sugar is rarely used at more than 20% of the malt in weight.

65

Brewers usually take their cane sugar as invert sugar. It has been diluted with water and a weak solution of sulphuric acid; the molecules of the sucrose become rearranged as equal quantities of glucose and fructose, by taking up one molecule of water.

$$C_{12}H_{22}O_{11} + H_2O \rightarrow C_6H_{12}O_6 + C_6H_{12}O_6$$

cane sugar   water   glucose   fructose

GLUCOSE AND FRUCTOSE HAVE THE SAME MOLECULAR STRUCTURE.

It is filtered, neutralised and evaporated into solid invert sugar after the process. I have always considered it a way of selling breweries some water! Invert sugar starts to ferment marginally more quickly, but is not worth bothering about as the enzymes of yeast "invert" sugar into glucose and fructose in the fermentation anyway.

.

TWO BEST BITTER MALT EXTRACT BREWS

My preference for brewing with malt extract is to use a good Golding hop, now freely available in homebrew shops.

Brew 1
1.045 Original Gravity
  100% Malt
  7 lb Malt Extract
  2½ oz Golding Hops
  2 oz Mag. Sulph. (Epsom Salts)

Brew 2
1.045 Original Gravity
  Malt & Sugar
  4¾ lb Malt Extract
  2 lb sugar
  2½ oz Golding Hops
  2 oz Mag. Sulph. (Epsom Salts)

Method for each brew
Use a large boiling vessel to boil the hops in 26 pints of water for

one hour. Boil vigorously with hops free in the water. Stir from time to time to disperse hops. Ten pints of water will evaporate. Pour into a suitable vessel through a fine nylon filter to remove hops. Clean remainder of hops from large boiling vessel. Return hopped water into this and dissolve malt extract (also sugar in Brew 2); add Epsom salts, bring to boil stirring to avoid malt extract burning. Boil for 10 minutes.

Have fermenting vessel ready with about 15 pints of cold water in. Cool the boiled solution (covered) in a sink full of water. Pour into fermenter, top up with water to the 5 gallon mark. Add yeast while topping up. Keep covered during fermentation. I use 1½ oz of fresh local brewery yeast but if not available, use a sachet of dried beer yeast.

The malt brew will ferment to a 'stop position' of S.G. 1009–1010 and the malt and sugar brew to 1008–1009. Bottle with ½ teaspoonful of sugar per pint or keg with a sterile solution of 5 oz sugar. Only the added priming sugar will ferment initially to give condition. I have had a 5 gallon keg of this beer 'on tap' for four months using gas entirely produced by the beer to maintain CO_2 protection and the pressure for dispensing. In both beers I use and recommend a liquid isinglass fining to ensure quick and lasting clarity.

The high proportion of malt and hops give this beer a fine creamy head and because of the body of the small remaining gravity, this head lasts and 'laces' the glass as you drink – a true 'real ale'!

Sugar is the most convenient material to add in priming to achieve a small secondary ferment in bottle or keg to give sparkle and head and, particularly in keg, to give the necessary pressure to dispense and the protective cover of CO_2 gas.

While malt, with hops for bitterness, will always be the main ingredient of beer there is a range of adjuncts which are often used in commercial brewing. Many are used to cut costs without any real benefit to the beer, but will make slight changes in flavour and fermentation. These may or may not be acceptable and may even be incorporated for a specific reason. In the last instance some adjuncts are absolutely necessary to achieve, for example, the black colour and unique flavour of Irish stout. I will therefore try to classify various adjuncts.

COLOURED MALTS

Normal malted barley, with varying degrees of kilning to give high or low tint, give the pale ale, bitter or amber coloured beers. But the dark beers, brown ales and stouts obtain their colour from roasted malts and the various kinds of these are black, brown, amber and crystal.

With the exception of crystal malt, all are made by roasting, to various degrees of caramelisation, normal kilned malt. Care must be taken to caramelise and not to burn or carbonise the malt. Caramelisation takes place at 445°F and carbonisation at 480°F and over. The enzymic activity of these malts will have been destroyed in the roasting and therefore they will have to rely on the enzymic action of the normal malt with which they are mashed to yield their fermentable sugars to the brew.

The non-mashing homebrewer should lightly crush coloured malts and mash them in a strong solution of a diastatic malt extract at 150°F for about one hour. As a rough guide, a stout would need about 30% of its ingredients as black malt and a brown ale, about 20% as brown or crystal malt.

CRYSTAL MALT

Crystal malt is made by the saccharification of the starch inside the husk of the barley at the "green malt" stage of malting, by steeping in water at 150°F. After this conversion to sugars, the still whole grain is roasted and a crystalline sugar is formed inside the corn.

Crystal malt is a very useful adjunct for the homebrewer, as it will be seen that no conversion is required and it is readily soluble as a fermentable sugar. It imparts a rich, full flavour to beer but should not be used in excess of 10% of materials.

Extract values of coloured malts are:–

Black malt – 85 brewers lb per barrel (36 gallons) per 336 lb.

Brown malts, amber and crystal – 86–90 brewers lb per barrel per 336 lb.

ROAST BARLEY

The roasting of unmalted barley is a common practice in the production of stouts and, apart from the economy of eliminating the malting process, it gives a dryer flavour to stout without the richer flavour of roasted malts. It requires conversion to sugars as described for coloured malt above.

Extract value when conversion has been achieved is 80 brewers (brs) lb per barrel per 336 lb.

GRITS

Rough, milled rice or maize grits are widely used in Japanese and American brewing. They have not been cooked, so have to be prepared by being gelatinised by boiling in a separate vessel and this sludge is mixed in with the mash, where it is converted by malt diastase.

FLAKED CEREALS

The use of flaked maize, barley and rice has come about purely as an economy but they, and sugar, can only replace a proportion of the malt-derived sugars in a brew and they require the diastatic or enzyme activity of the malt to convert them to fermentable sugars. It is a common mistake of homebrewers to include flakes of some sort of grain without conversion when boiling up a brew and I have seen flakes used in wine recipes. They will only add gelatinised starch, with all its troubles, to the fermentation.

Flaked cereals are manufactured by removal of husk and the oily germ (cooking oil is made from this); the remaining starch is cooked and gelatinised and then passed through heated rollers to dry off into thin flakes. When incorporated in a brewery mash they are readily converted to sugar by the malt diastase.

Again, the homebrewer who does not mash may mix flakes with a diastatic malt extract solution at 150°F, when conversion should take place in about one hour.

Some points about using flaked cereals are:–

Flaked maize: will 'dry' flavour when a full malty flavour is not required.

Flaked barley: improves head retention and gives a fuller flavour.

Flaked rice: Often used in lager brewing to give a thin dry flavour.

When full conversion of flakes is achieved, a slightly lower final gravity than an all malt brew after fermentation will result.

Extract values of flaked cereals:–
Flaked maize: 110 brs lb per barrel per 336 lb.
Flaked barley: 90 brs lb per barrel per 336 lb.
Flaked rice: 115 brs lb per barrel per 336 lb.
Grits or flakes should not be more than 15% of the total mash.

WHEAT FLOUR

This is another economy material that has been used by breweries in recent years. It does improve head retention in the finished beer, but to my mind imparts a soft, soapy taste if used to excess.

The only real reason for its use is to cut costs. Again, it relies on malt diastase to convert into fermentable sugars and the brewers introduce it by dusting it into their malt as the grist flows from the mill to the mash.

The homemasher should dust about 5% on to his crushed malt before mashing and the non-masher should dust it on to a solution of diastatic malt extract at 150°F and mix it in carefully to avoid lumps of flour with dry centres. It will replace an equal quantity of malt or flakes.

RAW GRAIN

Some brewers do use a small proportion of raw grain, barley or wheat, in their mash without prior preparation, but adjust proportions and use extra enzymes to ensure conversion. There is no advantage for the homebrewer in trying this as it is only an economy measure.

DOMESTIC PRODUCTS

I have seen many homebrew recipes incorporating the many domestic breakfast cereals on the market, such as corn flakes, bran flakes or Weetabix, but this practice is wrong if they, also, are not part of a malt mash or mixed with a diastatic malt extract solution for elimination of their starch. They have been cooked and taste fairly pleasant when milk and sugar are sloshed on them but they are only at the gelatinised starch state and need conversion to sugar to be of any more use and without this are merely a hazard in the shape of starch haze and poor fermentability to your beer or wine. The use of unmodified grain adjuncts is usually decided on as a cost saver to the brewer and I do not set much store on them, but the homebrewer might like to experiment. But do remember that their starch will not convert to useful sugars on their own or just by being added to a boiling of extract and sugars.

SUGARS

All the sugars are freely soluble and therefore need no conversion by enzymes. We have covered sucrose previously, and invert sugar; typical household sugar is the type available to homebrewers and is completely satisfactory. I have a preference for the sugar sold by Tate & Lyle which is refined from cane.

As sugar became more expensive to the brewer than malt, he changed to glucose, which he can obtain at a much lower price and it gives him an inexpensive supplement to sugars extracted from his malt mash. Glucose dries the palate of beer and is not quite as fermentable as sucrose, but the homebrewer can replace sugar with glucose without much difference.

Glucose is manufactured from cereal starch, mainly maize; like flaked maize, husks and germs are removed and the starch is then hydrolised into sugar by acids. It is then neutralised with an alkali and liquid corn sugar is the result, after filtration and concentration to a syrup. This syrup can be seeded with a minute addition of an abrasive, which will start a crystallising action. This spreads throughout the product and the final result is available to the homebrewer, broken up into glucose chips.

All the sugars, sucrose or glucose (in syrup or crystallised form), while being fully fermentable, contain no protein and therefore do not supply any yeast feeding properties which, in beer, is provided by the malt or malt extract.

Extract value of glucose:
Solid: 75 brs lb per barrel per 224 lb.
Syrup: 73 brs lb per barrel 224 lb.

BARLEY SYRUP

Barley syrup is a comparatively new material. It is made from the unmalted barley but husk, germ and starch are all used, unlike corn syrups. The conversion is made by mashing the barley with similar enzymes, commercially produced, that naturally occur in malting and mashing; a wort is produced which corresponds in all respects to malt wort. This is concentrated to a syrup and will replace malt, as it has all the yeast-feeding protein not contained in sugars and ferments to the same pattern as malts.

Extract value of barley syrup: 70 brs lb per barrel per 224 lb.

CARAMEL

Widely used to adjust the tint of beers and in some cases to change beer from a light ale to a brown ale! The homebrewer can burn household sugar to obtain caramel, or use gravy browning as this also is only caramel. It is not commercially produced by burning but by boiling a glucose syrup with ammonia and, by altering the process, caramels of varying tints and flavours, from acrid to luscious, are produced.

OTHER ADJUNCTS

We have now covered the main adjuncts used in brewing but, of course, there are many minor ones. I have dealt with finings but I have omitted such things as Irish moss as an auxiliary fining, also yeast nutrients, protein stabilisers (papain and proteolytic enzymes), heading agents and a host of other nostrums, because they are unnecessary. They are really 'medicines' for sick, badly-produced beer and we are not aiming at that!

We have come to the end of the broad fundamentals of brewing and I will continue with individual types of beers, stouts and lagers both commercially and for the homebrewer.

CHAPTER 9

A Traditional Country Brewery

I thought it would be of interest to visit a typical traditional brewery. For this I chose the brewery of Geo Gale and Co Ltd, at Horndean, Hampshire.

The brewing director is Mr Edward Argyle who has been a friend of mine for 30 years or so and I was always happy to supply my company's malt products to Horndean before my retirement. It was a pleasure to spend a day "putting a brew through" recently and endeavouring to illustrate this.

Like so many English breweries, Gales started as a small brew-house in a public house – in this case the Ship & Bell Hotel on the busy main London to Portsmouth road. This was in 1730 and as the popularity of the beer spread and more local houses wished to buy Gale's beer, a new brewery was built on the opposite side of the road. This covered their needs until the mid-19th Century, when it was destroyed in a fire.

At this time, the Industrial Revolution was in full swing, with an increase in population even in country districts, plus the expansion of Portsmouth and Southampton. So Gale's decided to build a new brewery beside the Ship & Bell Hotel. This was completed in 1869 and remains to this day. Although plant and machinery has been renewed over the years, it still is a completely traditional brewery noted for its splendid draught ales which probably have won more prizes at the Brewers Exhibition than any brewery.

Their main beers are their "ordinary", or BBB, a bitter beer of 1.037 gravity which is high for what they call "boy's bitter". Their Special Bitter was introduced in 1959 with a gravity of 1.055 (the standard gravity on which beer duty is calculated. A 20 brewers lbs beer). This was found to be too strong for their customers to have a "night out" on! – and was reduced to 1.051 in 1963 and is so today.

73

Gales Brewery, Horndean, Hampshire and "Brewery Tap" – the Ship and Bell Hotel.

There are not many so-called best bitters about with a gravity of 1.051 and it is a superb beer.

They also brew an amber coloured mild of 1.030 gravity and a dark mild at 1.032 for certain areas.

A unique, and very traditional beer is Gales Prize Old Ale, a barley wine of 1.095 gravity, which after maturation in storage vessels is conditioned naturally in cork stoppered bottles.

All these beers are brewed individually. The greater part of the output is sent out as naturally conditioned draught ale in metal casks (better than wood) to the 102 pubs now owned by Gales and also to free trade outlets. A proportion of the same brews are routed to the modern bottling and kegging department for conditioning and filtration as keg and bottled beer.

A DAY OUT

I left my home at Reading at 5.30 in the morning to be at Horndean before 7 a.m.; when the mash is put in. I was in time and beside the mash tun I found duty brewer Ken Leonard checking that the tun had been warmed up by steam by Peter Boyd, mash and copper foreman, who had started at 6.30! Mash liquor (water) was also checked and at 7 o'clock the slide of the grist hopper was opened, also the liquor valves and water and malt met in the mashing machine and the sweet, malty smell of the mash arose as the mix splashed on to the filter plates covering the bottom of the tun. The grist had been milled into the grist case the previous day and was best quality pale malt with an addition of 5% flour pellets, which in this form mix evenly throughout the grist. This is necessary for the diastase of the malt to convert the flour to sugars in the mash.

To make certain of full conversion of the flour, the malt is assisted during mashing by a gradual introduction of a solution of diastatic malt extract at mash temperature. When the mash was all in, mechanical rakes were sent round for one revolution to give a thorough mix. Mash temperature was taken and found to be the necessary 150°F. The mash is allowed to stand for about 1 hour while everyone has breakfast, then taps are set and sparging begins.

In Gale's mash tun, the usual rotating sparge arms are not used, but a stationary perforated ring of stainless tubing above the mash sprays the malt. Underneath the tun, the taps are opened and the sweet malt wort flows into a receiving vessel where a small proportion of invert sugar is added. With sparge and taps flowing well, Peter starts pumping the wort up to the copper boiling vessel, situated on the same level as the mash tun. Steam coils start heating the wort further as the copper fills up.

By noon, the gravity of the runnings from the mash are down to about 1.002 and taps are shut off. All that remains in the receiver is pumped to the copper. A mixture of Golding and Fuggle hop pellets are added to the copper, which is then closed down and the steam heater with fountain circulator is turned on and the brew is boiled for 1½ hours.

The large valve at the base of the copper is opened and the boiled hopped wort rushes into the circular 'hop back' vessel, creating the whirlpool effect and causing trub and hop debris to form as a cone on the filter plates of the hop back. The wort is promptly pumped up to a large, shallow, open cooling vessel at the top of the brewery. These vessels are rarely seen nowadays, but there is a great deal to be said in favour as a further deposit of 'hot break' unwanted protein is left in the vessel as the wort flows on and over upright heat exchangers or refrigerators.

The wort, now at 60°F, is pumped up into the fermenting room where one of the vessels is ready, clean and sterile, for the day's brew. As the fermenting vessel fills, the required yeast, pressed from previous brews and kept in air conditioned and refrigerated storage, is added. Hot water follows the wort through the plant to avoid any losses and also to adjust gravity in the fermenting vessel. When this is correct the "charge", as the brew is now called, is entered in the excise book and will be checked later by the local excise officer; the bill for duty will follow!

Gale's yeast is moderately flocculant and ferments without recourse to rousing. Looking around the fermenting room, I saw beers in various stages of fermentation. Yesterday's brew had the still fluffy remains of the earlier 'rocky' head, while the brew before that had formed a good thick 'crop'; an earlier brew had fermented to about 1.010 and the thick head was being skimmed off by suction, to be pressed for future use – a small amount for brewery fermentation, but the surplus for sale, probably to make Marmite.

After skimming, a protective cover of yeast is formed, about an inch or two deep, and the beer remains in this state, losing a further two or three degrees of gravity. About one week after brewing, it will be let down through a racking machine (a tank with three cask-filling hoses), where draught ale casks, with added finings, are filled. The draught ale is cellared for about a week before, bright and in condition, it is delivered to trade outlets.

A proportion of the beer from the fermenting vessels will go to storage tanks for conditioning and filtering prior to kegging or bottling.

The brew had gone through without the slightest hitch and made the process appear simple and easy, but this is because all the operators know their job. Mash temperatures are right and so is the ratio of liquor to malt. The wort flows easily from correctly set taps; boiling, hopping and cooling depend on the right setting of valves and experienced hands see to this at all stages.

The whole operation is discreetly overlooked by head brewer Derek Lowe, who also has at his disposal a well-staffed, modern laboratory for quality control. There is constant monitoring that pH is correct at all stages, yeast reproduction and yeast count at racking is normal, bacteriological control is adequate and yields, flavours and bittering are as wanted.

Gale's know exactly the beer they want, which has been decided by experience over the years, so the laboratory also checks all incoming materials for conformity with the specifications that Gale's have laid down.

The prize winning beers of Gale's of Horndean represent the best of traditional methods, combined with the best of modern technology and their success is well deserved.

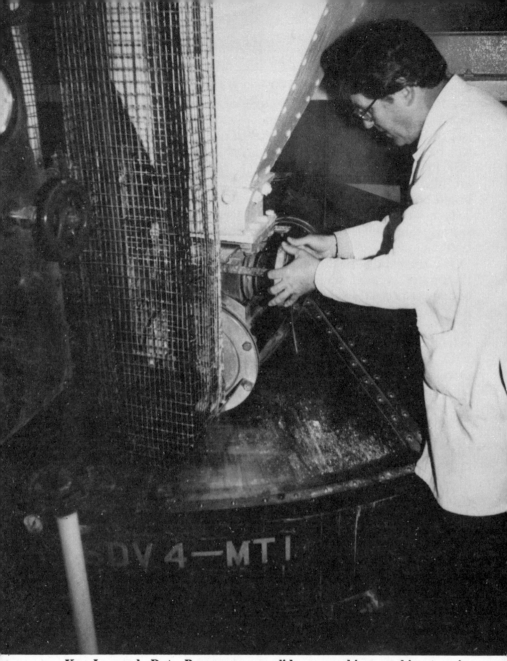

Ken Leonard, Duty Brewer, opens slide on mashing machine to mix crushed malt and hot water.

78

Above: Mash made up and being stirred with rotating rakes. One of the jets can be seen which later will spray hot water through the mash.

Below: After conversion taps are opened under the mash tun and sweet, fermentable, wort flows on for boiling with hops.

Peter Boyd adding hop pellets as wort approaches the boil.

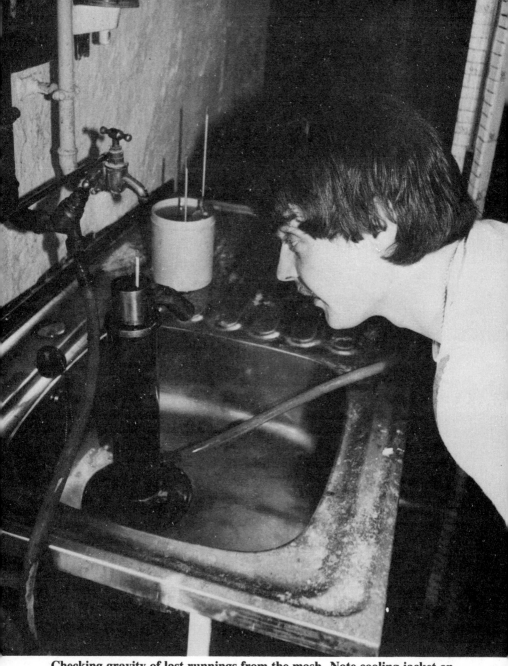

Checking gravity of last runnings from the mash. Note cooling jacket on sample jar.

Above: Wort cooling as it flows over refrigerator.

Below: Interior of "hop back" vessel showing filter plates to hold back spent hops.

Above: Wort from hop back pumped to open cooling vessel.

Below: Fermenting vessel ready for cooled wort. Note cooling coils or attemperators to control fermentation temperature.

Above: Cooled wort collected in fermenting vessel where yeast has been added.

Below: First "rocky" yeast head forms in about 10 to 12 hours.

Above: Fermentation complete: yeast crop has been skimmed off by suction take off shown and beer is let down for racking.

Below: Racking beer into cask to be sold as draught ale.

The Berkshire Brewery. The 16 insulated and weather proofed conical fermenters are seen in the centre.

CHAPTER 10

The Most Modern Brewery in Europe

In the middle of the 19th century there were many hundreds of small breweries throughout Britain serving the growing population caused by the Industrial Revolution and nearly every town and even small villages had a local brewery. Early in the 20th century a process began where the most successful breweries acquired their weaker brethren and this went on at increasing speed in the 1920s and 30s leading to the formation of large regional breweries.

H. & G. Simonds of Reading was typical of these. Founded in 1785 by W. B. Simonds as a small town brewery, it prospered and expanded in the 19th century and in 1885 became the limited company of H. & G. Simonds to attract public investment for further expansion and between 1919 and 1939 acquired breweries at Plymouth, Bristol, Staines, Cirencester, Brixham, Bridgend (South Wales), Blandford and Newbury. Further acquisitions after the 1939–45 war at Swindon, Torquay, another at Plymouth, Penzance and Newport (South Wales) made H. & G. Simonds the largest brewery company in the South West.

In the later post war period there has occurred the amalgamation of these large regional groups into giant national concerns and Simonds linked up with two other similar, old established groups, Courage of London and Barclay Perkins of London. At first it was a trading agreement with Courage and Barclay but in 1960 a full merger as Courage, Barclay & Simonds Ltd was completed and the whole group now trades as Courage Ltd. They in turn were acquired by Imperial Tobacco and are now the Brewery Division of the Imperial Group, a vast organisation embracing a huge variety of products.

Courage now had 4 large breweries in London, Reading, Bristol and Tadcaster and medium sized breweries at Plymouth and

Newark on Trent. With a rising demand for their beers and the new demand for lager a decision was made to build a completely new brewery on a 'green field' site capable of brewing the whole range of their well known English beers as well as lagers.

A site was chosen on the outskirts of Reading adjacent to the M4 and the building of the Berkshire Brewery was started in 1976; in 1980 the first brews went into trade.

THE BERKSHIRE BREWERY

The new brewery is undoubtedly one of the most modern breweries in Europe at this time and looked at from the M4 motorway it does not resemble in any way the older type, tall, "tower" breweries and could be confused with any other factory engaged in a variety of processes. Inside it is also not readily recognisable as a brewery. Do not be misled by this. It is a magnificent brewery and the age-old process of brewing still continues but is carried out in ultra-modern plant electronically controlled.

The first thing one notices is that it is a 'dry' brewery. In the old style breweries the brewer was splashed by the mash as he put it in the tun, the wort flowed out of the taps into the underback, the hopped boiled wort was seen pouring into the hop back and in the fermenting vessel the cooled beer flowed in and yeast was mixed and pitched into the beer. The Berkshire brewery is 'dry' because every process takes place in closed vessels and moves on through piping to the next vessel or container. In fact the first time any liquid is seen is when beer is put into glass in the pub. (There are, of course, points where samples are taken.)

The whole brewing operation is controlled from the console in the brewhouse which also gives a visual display of what is happening. At the touch of a switch a solenoid at some remote position will operate a valve and a flow of water, beer, yeast, malt, or sugar will take place, displayed and measured on the console, pumps and motors are motivated where this is required.

A whole brewing sequence can therefore be controlled from the console by one operator, from moving the required amount of malt from bulk storage, grinding, mashing, hopping, boiling, cooling, transferring to conical fermenter and, later, on to conditioning tanks and racking. The brew can also be entirely automated when a 'recipe disc', with the amounts of materials, times etc, is fed into the computer which programmes the console to control the brew. All plant can be operated manually should any failure occur in the automated control.

The internal layout of the brewery is immaculate and the stainless steel vessels, tiled walls and ceramic tiled floors are a great sight when viewed from the walkways through the brewery where Courage like to show visitors their fine brewery. Externally a programme of landscaping will make the brewery blend into the surroundings at a future date.

THE PROCESS

The brewing process is completely traditional although done in modern plant with automated control and it is also extremely flexible and can brew any type of beer, stout or lager.

Malt is delivered in bulk to nineteen malt silos. Malt is ground and held in grist cases above two mashing vessels. The grist is mashed into a mashing vessel where it remains for 2 to 3 hours for the conversion of malt starch to sugars. The mash is then pumped to a lauter tun where a sparge of hot water washes the sugars or wort from the malt husk and on to the boiling vessel (still called 'a copper' although made of stainless steel!) where hops are added.

The boil is for about 2 hours and then the hopped wort is pumped to a 'whirlpool' vessel where centrifugal force makes a cone of hop debris and malt protein which is held back while the hopped wort is pumped through a heat exchanger and on to one of a battery of conical fermenters where yeast is added. Fermentation time is variable to suit different beers but when complete the vessel is cooled and the yeast deposits in the bottom 'cone' shape of the vessel to be pumped away for cold storage in closed vessels. The spent grain in the lauter tun and the spent hops in the whirlpool are pumped out for disposal as by-products and the vessels are cleaned and sterilised by 'in place' cleaning systems. This also applies to fermenting vessels when the yeast has been pumped away and the beer passed on to conditioning tanks prior to kegging, bottling or loading into road tankers for other depots.

It is all quite logical and the flexibility and control of the brewing is complete. From the bulk storage of malts, hops, sugars and yeast any brew combination can be selected and put through with exact control of time and temperature. Be the brew ale or lager the method and raw materials will be right and when in the conical fermenters, the ideal fermenter for ale or lager, the correct yeast, fermentation times and temperatures will be applied and later conditioning and storage is accurately controlled.

The Berkshire Brewery really is a great brewery but I hope the homebrewer will realise that he is doing the same thing when he mashes a few lbs of lager or ale malt and boils them with his hops and watches his temperatures and exclusion of air while fermentation takes place.

Courage merely does it on a huge scale with sophisticated brewery engineering and fully automated control of process and throughput backed up by laboratory quality control of all materials, yeast and finished beers.

Part of Brewhouse showing console and one of the coppers in left foreground. A grist hopper above mash vessel in right background.

Above: The two mash vessels. Malt and hot water are mashed into these. The mash is pumped into the Lauter Tun for sparging and separating sweet wort from grain husk.

Below: The Lauter Tun. A filter bottom holds back husk while a vigorous sparge of hot water washes out the sweet wort.

One of the stainless steel "coppers" where the sweet wort is boiled with hops.

WHIRLPOOL

The whirlpool: boiled hopped wort from the copper enters in a circular stream for spent hops and malt protein to form a cone in centre.

Heat Exchanger. Clear boiled wort from whirlpool is cooled passing through the heat exchanger.

The base of the Conical Fermenters. When fermentation is complete the beer is cooled which causes yeast to deposit in the cone to be pumped away for cold storage. Beer follows on to conditioning tanks.

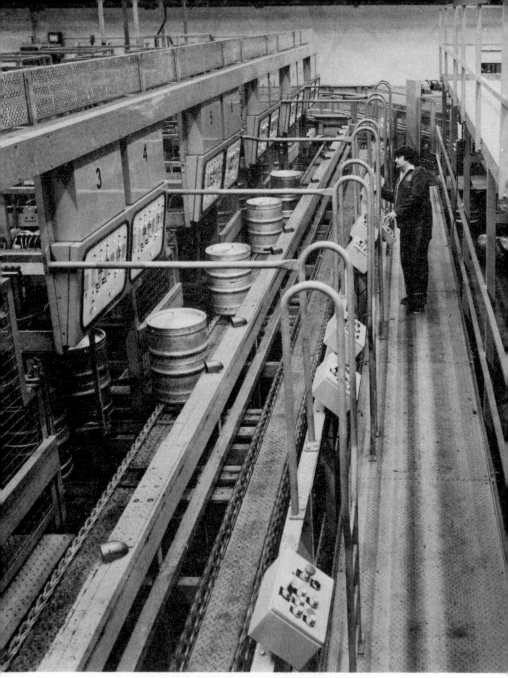

Kegging line for finished beer.

CHAPTER 11

Light Ale and Lager

So far I have described the brewing of a 1045 gravity best bitter with three formulations – (1) 100% grain malt, (2) 100% malt extract and (3) malt extract and sugar. In all three a good hop rate of 2½ oz per 5 gallons was used.

Very slight changes are required to produce different types of beer – so it is with **light ale**. This is a common type of beer, usually goes in bottle as light ale or perhaps under a house name, in draught as light bitter and, in keg, usually with a name.

It is pale in colour and low in original gravity, usually 1032–1035. With this gravity the brewer will pay less duty and the beer will be cheaper in the pub. It is a light, refreshing thirst quencher with about a 2½–3% alcohol content depending on to how low a gravity it has been fermented. The brewer will probably take it from the same mash as his best bitter and make up a strong copper for the best and a weaker copper for the light, with a reduced hop rate in the weaker boil, as not so much bittering will be lost in the lower gravity fermentation as a light ale need not be strongly hopped.

HOMEBREW LIGHT ALE

The homebrewer therefore need only adjust his materials to change his best bitter to a light ale, as in the following recipes:–

5 gallons
1035 gravity

MASHED MALT	**MALT EXTRACT**
4 lb pale malt	3½ lb light malt extract
2 lb sugar	2 lb sugar
1¼ oz hops	1¾ oz hops

Use the methods for mashing, boiling and fermentation previously described. Both beers should ferment to a 'stop position', or final gravity, of about 1004 to 1005. Bottle or keg with normal rate of priming sugar.

LAGER

Why do I couple light ale and lager? – It is because in my opinion, with the exception of a few premium brands the 'run of the mill' lagers now so heavily marketed are merely Continental type light ales. They are often brewed in the UK under licence from a European parent, given a fancy Germanic name and although they only pay a similar duty as a typical low gravity light ale with equally priced raw materials and, nowadays, equal production costs, they obtain a premium price from the willing consumers! The price of an article is what it sells for and if you like lager, and they are very pleasant tasting beers, you "pays the money".

LAGER BREWING

The very simple British infusion method of mashing has always depended on the well-modified malt from choice English barley, which presents no problems in conversion to fermentable sugars. The British brewer has always just mashed and washed the wort away from the husk.

The Continental brewers have traditionally only had available badly modified, hard and steely, higher protein malts from small-grained six row barleys. The word lager is German for storehouse and lager-bier is described as "a light beer kept for up to six months before use". No brewing genius sat down and invented lager. It has evolved through generations and the somewhat complicated decoction system of mashing, low temperature fermentation and storage period has been dictated by raw materials, the result of decoction and climate.

The decoction system of mashing usually requires three vessels – a mash vessel, a mash kettle and a lauter vessel. A mash would be made up at about 100°F in the mash vessel and, after an hour at this temperature, about one third is pumped to the mash kettle where it is raised to 149°F and later mixed back into the main mash, bringing the whole up to around 122°F. A second third of this mash is then taken into the kettle and boiled for half an hour and returned to the mash tun, bringing the whole to about 150°F for saccharification. A further third is taken to the kettle and boiled and then returned to the mash to bring it to about 180°F for stabilisation. The mash tun and mash kettle have propellers for mixing and stirring.

After this performance, the mash is pumped over to the lauter vessel, which has a filter bottom, and the wort is washed out for boiling with hops. This was a triple decoction but there were also double decoction and single decoction mashes, all aimed at bringing the mash through a series of temperature changes for protein degradation and saccharification.

The modern lager brewery merely has a mash vessel with stirring gear and heating ability to produce a range of temperatures before the mash is pumped over to a lauter vessel for filtering out the wort. This wort is boiled with Continental hops and these hops, such as Hallertau and Saaz, are the key flavour-makers in lager beer.

After cooling, the beer is fermented. Lager fermentations have always used yeasts which are active at about 50°F and although called "bottom fermenting" they do make the usual "cauliflower heads" as top yeast does and the yeast is most active at this time. The heads fall back to leave a firm covering on the lager. When fermentation is finished, the lager is rapidly cooled down to about 42°F, when the yeast will precipitate to the bottom of the vessel. This is very similar to the performance of yeast in the conical fermenters used in modern Britain ale breweries.

After fermentation, the lager goes on to low temperature storage. This was absolutely necessary and really was dictated by the amount of haze-forming protein extracted by the decoction mash and the poor malt used. Storage began at 40°F and yeast was added to provide gas and condition initially. Cooling would continue down to about 35°F when the gas created would go into solution.

Ten weeks was a normal lager period; during this time the colloidal protein would clear from the lager and it became "chillproof" and, thus, at one time it was the only beer which could be chilled without forming a chill haze. Nowadays, all bottled beers are chilled before filtration and all can be kept in a cool, chilled condition.

Lager is a far more universal beer than British ale and is brewed in most countries of the world, to the exclusion of other types. The ingredients used are variable. In Germany, their beer purity laws forbid the use of sugar and any protein stabilisers but they are allowed up to 20% of cereal only adjuncts, such as flaked maize, rice or barley, which will be converted in the mash by malt enzymes. Sugar is used in other countries particularly corn (maize) sugar in America.

Various "odd" lagers are produced, such as malt liquor, where a high proportion of sugar leads to a zero or lower final gravity. This principle is also used for slimming lagers, where a higher proportion of sugar plus the enzyme amyloglucosidase is used to ferment out all sugars. The slimmers should realise the hoax in this because alcohol is as high in calories as sugar. Similarly, the diabetic lagers rely on fermenting out all sugars, but the sufferer must balance against the alcohol.

There has been a huge growth in lager drinking in Britain and from almost nil 20 years ago, it now has about 30% of the market. Most large modern breweries produce lager in the same plant that produces their pale ales, bitters and milds, and will have a mash vessel where temperature changes can be applied (if thought necessary) before going on to a lauter tun, or perhaps a Strainmaster or mash filter for wort separation.

The conical fermenter is ideal for lager or ale and all breweries have cold storage tanks for all beers, not only lager, for protein stabilisation before bottling or kegging.

It would be too much to expect that a homebrewer could go through the true lager process, but he really has no need to do so to produce a reasonable lager.

Consider the lagering or cold storage. This was not done originally to enable Continental brewers to sell chillproof beer, it was done to eradicate the haze-producing proteins caused by the decoction system, which in itself was necessitated by the poor quality malt available. The malts now available to homebrewers eliminate any need for decoction mashing and therefore minimise haze problems. Low temperature yeast was only necessary to

100

create condition and gas in the cold storage period. I am not aware that there is a true lager yeast available in homebrew shops. If there is, it would be worth trying, but the generally available sachets of dried beer yeast are perfectly adequate, fermenting at 65°F, and are closer to lager yeast than they are to beer yeast.

Hops are the main contributor to the lager taste and good Continental hops are available in all homebrew retail outlets. I prefer Hallertau hops. The home lager brewer therefore has only to find a very pale malt or a pale malt extract. Lager malt is only malted English barley which has been lightly kilned and because of this is pale in colour and high in enzymes (diastase).

The colour of your lager may be lightened by including a little flaked rice, failing this, flaked maize, in the brew, which will also dry the final flavour to a typical lager palate. The flakes must be digested by the malt mash and in a malt extract brew must be converted by mashing them in a solution of the malt extract at 150°F for one hour.

LAGER 5 gallons	5 gallons PREMIUM LAGER
1035 gravity	1045 gravity
MASHED MALT	MASHED MALT
3½ lb pale malt	5 lb pale malt
½ lb flaked rice	½ lb flaked rice
2 lb sugar or glucose	2½ lb sugar or glucose
1½ oz Hallertau hops	2¼ oz Hallertau hops
MALT EXTRACT	MALT EXTRACT
3 lb diastatic malt extract	4 lb diastatic malt extract
½ lb flaked rice	½ lb flaked rice
2 lb sugar or glucose	2½ lb sugar or glucose
1½ oz Hallertau hops	2¼ oz Hallertau hops

It will be noticed that the quantity of sugar is above my normal practice. This is to lighten colour, dry the flavour and lead to a lower final gravity. In brewing, these lagers – both types, malt or malt extract – should be given a thorough boil to precipitate and eliminate protein.

Mashing temperature and method is the normal for beers with the rice in the mash, and hops should be boiled in the wort for one hour. In the malt extract lager, the rice must be converted in a solution of the malt extract at 150°F for one hour. During this, boil the hops for one hour in 20 pints water. Strain out the rice debris from malt and the hops from their boil. Mix the remaining malt extract and sugar with the hop water and boil for 20 minutes.

Make up to 5 gallons and ferment. The stop position (final gravity) will be about 1.003. Bottle or keg with normal rate of priming sugar.

With these materials and good boiling, a lager is produced which will be reasonably chill-proof with light chilling and provide a refreshing beer with a genuine lager palate.

CHAPTER 12

Brown Ale and Mild

Light-coloured bitter beers are nowadays the most universally popular on the British market and they are sold in a variety of types by local and national breweries in draught and keg form.

In the lower gravities, they will usually be called simply bitter or pale ale, while the higher gravity varieties will often be given a prestige name such as 'Abbot', 'London Pride', 'Director's Bitter' and many other excellent beers. They will have a higher price, as they have attracted a higher excise duty, which is levied on original gravity.

An interesting survival from the early days of British rule in India is the name India Pale Ale. This was a beer brewed strong enough to stand the long sea passage to India in an unpasteurised condition in cask.

The name persists in various beers called I.P.A. but unfortunately these are often only low gravity light ales.

Next in popularity is lager in bottle or keg form. Before the swing in public taste to bitter beer and lager, about half the output of British breweries was devoted to producing draught mild ale.

MILD ALE

A general description of mild ale would merely be that it is much darker in colour than bitter, does not have such a hop bitterness and, in consequence, has a sweet and bland flavour. It is easier to drink than bitter and it is fair to say that youngsters invariably started their drinking habits on mild but on maturity acquired the desire for the sharper taste of bitter beers.

There are the usual regional variations in mild ales. In London and the south of England, mild ale is invariably a dark beer, almost

103

black, but when held up to a light, is seen to be clear all through with a dark brown colour. In the West Midlands and the north of England a mild ale is not much different from the bitter in colour and could be described as amber-coloured but with a soft bland flavour.

Mild ales, originally always natural draught ales, found their way into bottle as chilled, filtered and pasteurised brown ales and, at higher gravities, as dark strong ales. A good example of a strong mild with the lighter northern colour is the famous Newcastle Brown.

Many breweries are now producing mild beers in keg and this beer lends itself well to the process of filtration, gassing and serving under pressure as a stabilised product. The coloured materials used give a keg mild an attractive creamy head and to my mind, make it a better drink than the old draught mild, which was often flat, permissible in a bitter with its sharper taste, but uninteresting with the soft flavour of mild.

BREWING MILD ALE

Originally, the brewing centres for mild were dictated by the local water and those waters coming from the chalky layers of the South and the London area were most suitable. Until 30 years ago the large London breweries were almost entirely used in brewing the universally drunk London Mild, while breweries with sulphated water, such as Burton on Trent, were more suitable for pale ales and bitters.

There is very little mild brewed in London and the south now and water treatment allows any beer to be brewed at any location. Brewers adjust their water, or 'liquor' as they call it, to the type of beer brewed by adding or subtracting the salts required. The brewer wishing to brew a mild would not be as concerned about carbonates in the water as a pale ale brewer and would add very much less sulphate than for pale ale or bitter. He would add a small amount of chloride (common salt), which has a marked effect in bringing out sweetness in the beer.

For 100 barrels (3,600 gallons) of 1040 gravity mild ale, a typical make-up would be: 10 quarters (2,240 lb) of mild ale malt, which is more highly kilned than pale ale malt and adds colour and flavour; 1 quarter (224 lb) of crystal malt, for sweetness and flavour; 1 quarter (224 lb) of brown or amber malt for further colour and flavour and 4 quarters (895 lb) of sugar. This sugar would be the darker No 3 invert or perhaps partially refined soft brown sugar.

These are the main ingredients to give the fermentable extract for the brew and it will be seen that it is a small change from our original malt bitter and colour is the real difference; but the hop rate is most significant and, while the earlier bitter brew required 1¼ lb of hops per barrel (36 gallons), this mild ale would have only 7/8 to 1 lb of hops per barrel and these would be of Fuggle variety rather than Golding.

Mashing, boiling and fermentation is standard British practice in whatever plant the brewery is using.

There are many variations of the above mild, such as slight variations for lighter or darker colours and higher or lower original gravities for weaker or stronger milds.

BROWN ALES

The mild ales brewed are sold as naturally conditioned milds or filtered and carbonated (CO_2 gas put in) and dispensed under this gas pressure as keg mild, but when put into bottle they are invariably sold as the quite popular brown ale. The sweetness of this beer is *not* obtained from the mashing and brewing process. Brown ales are usually made from fairly low gravity 1030–1035 mild ale brews, which ferment down to between 1003–1005 and thereby any sweetness has fermented away, leaving a fairly dry, dark beer. This is transferred to tanks in the bottling department where it is heavily primed with a sugar solution back to about 1015 gravity, dependent on the sweetness required.

This would normally start a violent secondary fermentation, so the beer is immediately filtered to remove any yeast. It would now be flat, so CO_2 gas is injected before it is put into bottle. After bottling, the beer is pasteurised to stop any possibility of fermentation. The sweetness in a bottle of brown ale is therefore due to the addition of unfermented sugar.

HOME BREW MILD

It is a simple operation for the homebrewer who prefers to mash grain malt to make up a mild ale. Using the calculations from "Weights and Measures" (Chapter 5) and extract values of adjuncts a good mild ale can be made as follows:–

5 gallons 1040
MASHED MILD ALE
  4 lb Mild Ale Malt
  ½ lb Crystal Malt
  ½ lb Brown or Amber Malt
  2 lb Brown Sugar
  1¾ oz Fuggle Hops
  A few drops caramel (gravy browning) if darker colour is wanted
  Treat with ¼ oz Magnesium sulphate and 1 oz common salt.

Mash in 2 gallons of water at 165°F to obtain a mash heat of 150°F (the malts will have been crushed before mashing) hold heat and stand for two hours. Use about 2 gallons or sparge water at 170°F to wash out and separate wort from mash and boil this with the sugar and hops for one and a half hours. Make up to 5 gallons in fermenting vessel and cool (covered) until temperature is down to 70°F, then introduce a sachet of dried beer yeast or 1½ oz of fresh brewery barm yeast if available. Final gravity will be from 1005–1008, when the mild ale may be bottled or kegged with normal sugar priming and liquid beer finings.

5 gallons 1040
MALT EXTRACT MILD ALE
  3 lb Dark Malt Extract
  ½ lb crystal Malt
  2 lb Brown Sugar
  1¾ oz Fuggle Hops
  A few drops caramel (gravy browning) to darken colour if desired.

106

Crush the crystal malt and dissolve in hot water. Strain to remove crystal malt husks. Add crystal water to 20 pints of water and boil hops in this for one hour. Add ¼ oz magnesium sulphate and 1 oz salt to this boil. Strain out hops and dissolve malt extract and sugar in hop water. Bring to boil, stirring to avoid burning the malt extract, and boil for 15 minutes.

Make up to 5 gallons in fermenting vessel and ferment as for mashed brew. This will also ferment to a final gravity of 1005–1008, when bottling or kegging as above may be carried out.

BROWN ALE HOME BREW

It is not really possible to brew a true commercial type brown ale in the home. We have seen that the sweetness of this beer is obtained by adding sugar after fermentation, but the filtration and pasteurising (and carbonating) which is then essential is beyond the ability and equipment of the most homebrewers.

Increasing the proportion of sugar in the recipe *never* produces sweeter beer, but only dries the flavour because of the lower final gravity as the added sugar ferments completely. A partial answer is to eliminate the 2 lb of sugar in the foregoing recipes and increase the malt and malt extract in either of the brews by 2 lb. The final gravity would then be about 1010 at bottling, which would give a fuller, sweeter beer.

Another partial solution would be to exchange only 1½ lb of sugar for malt or extract and add ½ lb of Lactose. Lactose (milk sugar) is used in very small proportions in some milk stouts and is not very sweet but is very unfermentable and will keep the final gravity a degree or so higher. When bottling or kegging, reduce the priming sugar slightly to ¼ tsp per pint to reduce secondary fermentation. To increase sweetness in bottle, the homebrewer can only resort to something which is not permitted to the commercial brewer and that is to add a non-fermenting sweetener such as saccharin. One or two tablets according to taste may be added when bottling and the homebrewer will end up with a good, sweet and malty brown ale.

The only extra ingredient for porter or stout is roast malt or roast barley;
an alternative is caramel (gravy browning).

CHAPTER 13

Porters and Stouts

We now move on to porters and stouts. I feel that considerable misleading information on these has found its way into the world of homebrewing – and this is backed up by the advertising of commercial stouts! The adverts suggest that there is some elusive magic or mystique surrounding their brewing. This is not so.

I have always stressed that beer is brewed from the sugars extracted from malted barley; these are boiled with hops and fermented. Only slight changes in materials and adjuncts and slight proportional changes of these, plus adjusting to a weaker or stronger beer by making original gravity higher or lower, results in a variety of beers.

So, it is with porters and stouts. They are perfectly normally brewed beers from standard malt and hops and the significant change is brought about by the addition of *colour*, by adding a small proportion of caramelised cereal in the mash or caramelised sugar in the boiling.

I did my initial training as a brewer in a brewery at Cardiff, which brewed three standard pale beers, an IPA (India Pale Ale) at 1048, a bitter at 1041 and a light bitter at 1035. From these three basic brews, no less than 13 different types of beer were sold from the brewery. This was done by the addition of caramel.

Each week, a solution of caramel at 1.110 gravity was made and excise duty was charged on this. This was added, in varying degrees, to subdivisions of the three brews. In draught form, the three went out as IPA, Bitter and Light Bitter and, coloured, as Strong Ale, Homebrew and Mild. This was repeated in the bottling department and six bottled versions were produced.

The 13th type was Oatmeal Stout in bottle and, for this, heavy colouring was added to the 1048 IPA. One pound of oatmeal was

109

always added to the IPA mash, which made no difference at all in the brew of 200 barrels but Excise insisted on it to enable us to use the word oatmeal on the label.

They were all excellent beers and the oatmeal stout was extremely popular. The 1048 IPA was a good, full drinking, hoppy bitter and the large addition of caramel, with its acridity, cut across the original flavour and made a really good stout.

The brewery was eventually taken over by a London brewery with a quite well known stout of their own and they threw up their hands in horror at the "IPA converted" product; it was withdrawn and their own was substituted. We were then inundated with letters of protest demanding that oatmeal stout be brought back!

I do not favour adding colour after fermentation in this way, but it was widely done and many proprietary conversion coloured sugars were available to brewers. My readers will have guessed that my normal homebrew is a 1045 gravity best bitter, a good malt and hops brew, always available with a creamy head under its own generated pressure from a keg in my larder.

A friend called who I knew was a great stout enthusiast. I drew off a small amount of my beer into a pint and stirred a small teaspoonful of gravy browning in this and then topped up the pint with the bitter. He thought it was a magnificent stout!

The colour, be it obtained from roast cereal or caramel, should be part of the boil before fermentation so that it will blend in with the total brew. A stout wort, gravity for gravity, is no more glutinous than any other beer. The colour obtained from the small proportion of roast cereal or caramel added is of the consistency of black ink, but with all dark beers more melanoidins are produced during the boil which increase surface tension of the final beer, leading to good creamy head formation and retention.

PORTER

Porter is simply a draught black beer which was once widely served in London and is indigenous in Ireland. It is lightly hopped and of modest gravity and was easy to produce and dispense in draught, as it had none of the problems of clarity nowadays required in light coloured beers.

Porter was a 'new' beer first brewed by brewer Ralph Harwood in Shoreditch in 1722 and probably by accident! The many small brewhouses in London were brewing beers with the brown malts of Hertfordshire and it is possible that Harwood received some malt burnt from over-kilning.

The resultant black beer was acceptable in flavour and, what is more important, was more stable than the paler beers which, at the state of knowledge at the time, were difficult to clear and store for any length of time. Storage was necessary; the brewers then did not brew in the hot summer months because, without knowledge of sterility and control, summer brews so often went turbid and sour. Porter kept well and even if it went a little cloudy, this was not noticed. The black beer became popular among the porters of the London markets and owes its name to this, but then became universally accepted; most London brewers took it up and Hertfordshire maltsters supplied the highly kilned porter malt.

It could be said that porter was the basis on which the large London breweries grew – and also the Irish breweries. It has virtually disappeared now, except in Dublin and other parts of Ireland, but a stronger version of porter was STOUT, named thus simply because the word stout is synonymous with strong. I feel that the homebrewer should not really concern himself with porter, but addition of colour to a mild ale provides a reasonable porter.

Porter brewing was the cause of the growth of the great London breweries and by about 1750 Samuel Whitbread, Henry Perkins (later Barclay Perkins) and Sir Benjamin Truman of Trumans Brewery, Brick Lane, had emerged as giants and were vying with each other to be the biggest porter brewers in London.

Porter lent itself to mass production and these brewers used their earlier profits wisely, to have the capital necessary to enlarge their plants and, what is more important, to build their vast 'porter tun rooms' or vat houses for storing and maturing their winter brewing of the stable beer porter. By the end of the 18th century, they had all also installed the new steam engines to drive, through shafting and belts, the malt mills, mashing machines and beer pumps, which had previously been powered by a horse wheel with several horses pulling in a circle.

There were, of course, many other porter brewers in London and the fame of London porter grew and it was sold throughout the country and exported. It is interesting to note that there was a large trade with Ireland, where porter was brewed but was not truly indigenous and the brewing was on a small scale.

GUINNESS

The Irish brewers soon rectified this and by 1800 the position was completely reversed, with almost no imports of English porter. This was now brewed for the Irish by Guinness of Dublin (and others) and Guinness had begun the phenomenal increase of the export of Irish porter, later the famous Guinness Extra Stout, into England. (By 1800, English brewers had started to change to pale beers).

By the 1930s, Guinness' trade led them to build a new large brewery at Park Royal, London. Although a modern and imposing brewery, fully mechanised, the brewing system remains that of a typical 18th century porter brewhouse. – Malt and roast barley produce a black wort to be boiled with hops, fermented without temperature control and on to maturation and blending of different aged stouts in the vast vat house.

The 18th century was the growth time for porter and the big brewery companies grew from this but the 19th century saw English brewing change to 'running' pale beers which did not require the accepted winter brewing and subsequent vatting and storage.

There were many causes for this. Malting techniques were improving and with this better quality control and an awareness of sterility requirements (although Pasteur had not yet demonstrated why), the cooling of fermentations with 'attemperator' coiled cold water pipes in the fermenting vessels and lastly the introduction of Isinglass finings for rapid fining and clarity.

So, the English style of brewing changed to the draught bitters, pale ales and milds which took about a week to brew and ferment and, after a brief cellarage in cask, were fined and went into trade. It has remained much the same with draught ales to this day and the huge porter vat houses have disappeared in English breweries, except at Park Royal, but the descendants of Samual Whitbread

112

kept their famous porter tun room in Chiswell Street, London, as a museum show piece and it is used as a conference room and banqueting suite.

The disappearance of porter style brewing did not stop English breweries making stouts of their own and most English, Welsh and Scottish brewers have a bottled stout among the various types of beer they sell. They are properly brewed, with the mash containing a proportion of coloured malt or barley, hopped according to taste required, fermented, cold-stored in tank, filtered and carbonated, bottled and pasteurised.

STOUT

Most breweries produce a stout of their own but the king of stouts must be the Irish stout Guinness, produced in Dublin and Park Royal brewery London. It is rare for me not to have a Guinness at lunch time especially in the winter because it is a unique and first class product and in bottle, one of the only two beers left which condition naturally in the bottle.

Guinness is a perfectly orthodox 100% cereal brew using no sugar, caramel, liquorice, enzymes or any other weird products or ideas! The main ingredient of Guinness is good quality mild ale malt; the colour is obtained from a small percentage of added roast barley which they roast themselves. Roast barley gives a whiter head than roast malted barley.

A small proportion of flaked barley is incorporated to enhance the creamy head but also probably for economic reasons and likewise a very small proportion of barley flour. The proportions of these materials are Guinness's secret, but I would assume about 80% malt 5% flaked barley and barley flour and 15% roast barley. These are mashed in the normal manner into mash tuns but Guinness call their tuns 'Kieves' and the diastase of the malt will convert itself and the unmodified roast barley, flakes and flour into a black wort which is boiled with hops and then cooled and fermented.

It is after fermentation that Guinness becomes unique, because the stout is transferred to large vats in an even larger vat house. At one end of the vat house is a vessel from which the road tankers and

113

other containers are filled. This vessel is made up with stouts of different ages.

Guinness does not brew different stouts but blends stouts of different ages. Into this blend some newly fermenting stout is added to start secondary conditioning. This is called gyling or 'Krausening' and the stout is rapidly transported to a brewery, where it will be bottled. In about a week it will have generated condition and it then goes to pubs and other outlets for sale.

Why is Guinness "good for you?" Apart from being a fine beer of good gravity (mid 40s) it has no more virtue than any other beer of similar gravity but it does have yeast in the bottle and yeast is an invaluable tonic. This cannot be said of draught Guinness in keg which is the same good stout but the yeast is filtered out and the beer is pressure dispensed by a mixture of CO_2 gas and nitrogen. The nitrogen helps to suppress excessive foaming, which occurred when the stout was dispensed under CO_2 alone and in no way helps in giving a head.

The fine creamy head of Guinness is created in the brewing with 100% cereal mash, which includes roast barley and flaked barley, a good hop rate (probably over 1 lb per barrel) and not fermenting to zero gravity. There is no hurry in the fermenting and vat house maturation of Guinness and a properly brewed beer will leave 1/5th to 1/6th of original gravity in the final beer. It would be a thin, characterless beer if this were not so and you will find a bottle of Guinness in good condition will have a remaining gravity of 1.005.

HOME BREW STOUT

It would be difficult for a home brewer to go through the maturation and blending of differently aged stouts as Guinness do, but something similar can be done by brewing one gallon every 10 days or so until you have five stouts. Start another and when fermenting take out a pint. Put the five one gallon brews into a keg and add the pint of working stout.

If you wish to try this, divide either of the following recipes by 5 and brew in one gallon batches.

5 gallon 1045
MASHED STOUT
  7 lb mild ale malt
  ½ lb flaked barley
  1 lb roast barley *OR* black malt
  2½ oz Fuggle hops

Mash the malt, flakes and roast barley in 2 gallons water at 165°F to obtain a mash heat of 150°F. Hold the heat and leave to stand for two hours. Use about 2 gallons of water at 170°F to wash out the wort from the mash. Boil this with the hops for one and a half hours. Make up to 5 gallons and cool (covered) to 70°F, before adding a sachet of dried beer yeast or 1½ oz of fresh brewery yeast. Final gravity will be about 1008. Bottle or keg with no more than ½ teaspoon of sugar per pint and use no finings.

5 gallon 1045
MALT EXTRACT STOUT
  6 lb diastatic malt extract
  ¼ lb flaked barley
  1 lb roast barley *OR* black malt
  2½ oz Fuggle hops

Make a small mash at 150°F with a pound of the malt extract and the flakes and roast barley. Hold for 2 hours at this temperature. Pour all the mash, the remainder of the malt extract and the hops into 20 pints of water and boil for one hour. Strain out the hop and barley debris. Make up to 5 gallons and ferment. The final gravity will be between 1005–1008. Keg or bottle as for mashed brew.

Guinness in bottle is a naturally conditioned beer containing yeast and it is well worthwhile culturing this for your brews. Buy a bottle of Guinness and shake it thoroughly. Pour this into a small container and add a sterile solution of 3 tablespoonfuls of malt extract dissolved in a half pint of water. Keep covered in the airing cupboard and in two to three days you should have increased the yeast sufficiently for a 5 gallon brew. Put all the yeast and liquid into your prepared brew and this can give a very authentic flavour.

SWEET STOUTS

They are pleasant beers to drink and are invariably sweeter tasting than the vatted and blended Guinness, which is finally naturally conditioned in the bottle. Each type has its devotees and the most well-known and universally sold sweet stout is **Mackeson**.

Mackeson was originally brewed by Mackeson & Co of Hythe, Kent. I first learnt about it in the early 1930s, when a traveller from the brewery called on the brewery where I was apprenticed, in Cardiff, asking us to stock it in our public houses. The bottle at that time had a silver label depicting a milk churn and it was called Mackeson's Milk Stout. The label also stated that it contained the equivalent of a certain quantity of milk – I have forgotten the quantity! Of course, no milk was used in the brew but the necessary amount of milk sugar or lactose was.

Labelling regulations eventually killed off this first label and it became Mackeson's Stout, but still bore the note about the equivalent of milk.

This has now also disappeared and it is plain Mackeson Stout. The brewery was taken over by Whitbread; they promoted the brew and made it the well-known national beer that it is today. It is a pleasant and unashamedly sweet and luscious stout.

The label states that it is 'specially brewed from the finest roast malt', but it will be a normal malt mash with a proportion of roast malt to give the black colour. This proportion would depend on the degree of roasting of the coloured malt used and this is Whitbread's secret. The black wort produced is boiled with hops and perhaps a small amount of sugar and, possibly, a very small amount of lactose. The hop rate does not appear to be high, thus preserving the soft, luscious flavour.

I would think the original gravity is in the high 30s or perhaps 1040. This ferments normally to a final gravity in fermenting vessel of between 1005 to 1010.

The stout is then removed to tank where it is heavily primed with a full-flavoured sugar, probably candy sugar, to a gravity of about 1020. The knowledgeable homebrewer will know this would normally start a further secondary fermentation. It is essential, therefore, that the stout is filtered to remove yeast, so some carbonating (gassing) would probably be required before bottling and pasteurisation. The pasteurisation might be done with a sterilising sheet filter or, if not, by pasteurisation in bottle. The homebrewer who buys a bottle of Mackeson will find, if he tests it with a hydrometer, that there is always between 1018 and 1020 final gravity in the stout, largely given by unfermented sugar, and this contributes more than anything to the luscious taste. That is why the advertisement is quite correct when it says 'It *looks* good and *does* you good', because a shot of sugar is the quickest way of giving energy and overcoming tiredness!

HOME BREW SWEET STOUT

We have said earlier, when looking at sweet brown ale, which is also sweetened by sugar priming after fermentation, that the then essential filtration, carbonating and pasteurising is beyond the capability of the homebrewer. So it is with a stout primed to sweetness, but a soft flavoured stout is easy enough to brew at home. The only real change from a strong mild or brown ale is the addition of colour to the brew. With a sweet stout this is best done by including roast or black malt in the mash rather than roast barley.

MASHED SWEET STOUT
5 gallons 1040
  5 lb mild ale malt
  ½ lb crystal malt
  ½ lb roast black malt
  1 lb soft brown sugar
  1¾ oz Fuggle hops
  Treat water with ¼ oz magnesium sulphate and 1 oz common salt.

Crush the mild, crystal and black malts and mash in 2 gallons of water at 165°F to obtain the usual mash heat of 150°F. Hold the heat and stand for two hours. Use 2 gallons of sparge water at 170°F to wash out and separate wort from mash. A few drops of caramel may be added at this stage if sufficient colour has not been achieved.

Boil the wort and some added water with the hops and sugar for one to one and a half hours. Strain out spent hops and make up to 5 gallons in fermenting vessel at 70°F. Pitch with a sachet of dried beer yeast or 1½ oz of fresh brewery barm yeast if obtainable. Ferment as usual and final gravity will be between 1008–1010, when the stout may be bottled or kegged with normal sugar priming but fining is not really necessary.

MALT EXTRACT & CARAMEL STOUT
5 gallons 1040
    4 lb dark malt extract
    2 lb soft brown sugar
    8 fluid oz gravy browning (caramel E150)
    1¾ oz Fuggle hops

In my opinion, the colour required in a stout may be obtained from burnt sugar or caramel equally as that obtained from roast malt or barley, but should be included in the brew before fermentation. This malt extract and caramel stout is very easy to brew and makes a good enough stout.

Boil the hops in about 20 pints of water for one hour. Strain out spent hops and use the hopped water to dissolve the malt extract, caramel and sugar. Bring to boil, stirring to avoid burning the extract, and simmer for about 15 minutes. Make up with cold water to 5 gallons in fermenting vessel and ferment as the mashed brew and final gravity will also be between 1008–1010. Bottle or keg with normal sugar priming.

Both these stouts may be brewed stronger at 1045 original gravity by increasing malt or malt extract by ¼ lb.

Neither will be as sweet as commercial sweet stouts, as the home brewer cannot filter, prime heavily and pasteurise. As the freely fermenting sugars have fermented out, only the final gravity of unfermentable provides sweetness. If lactose sugar is available, about ¼ lb may be added to either brew at the boiling stage and will provide a slightly higher final gravity and possibly a sweeter palate, but it is not a great sweetener and is expensive.

As with sweet brown ale, the homebrewer will again have to do what the commercial brewer is not allowed to do and that is to add saccharin tablets according to taste when bottling. One or two per pint bottle will give an apparent sweetness and an enjoyable sweet stout will be achieved.

CHAPTER 14

Barley Wine

Now for that premium quality beer of the brewing industry, barley wine! In the many lectures I have given to homebrew and wine Circles I have invariably started my talk by saying, "Beer is made from barley but you *cannot* brew beer from barley".

I reiterate: nothing fermentable or valuable in brewing can be obtained from barley grains as they come from the fields. The barley has to be malted by steeping it in water, allowing the corns to germinate and start growing and then stopping the growth by kilning the sprouted barley over fire. Only then will the insoluble starch, which fills the centre of the grain, have been "modified" and made soluble so that the malted barley, or malt as it is now called, may be lightly crushed and mashed with hot water. The barley enzymes, which have been active in modifying the barley into malt, will continue their work in the mash and readily complete the starch breakdown into fermentable sugars of malt, which is the basis of all beer.

So it is with Barley Wine, which is not made from barley but from malted barley (malt). The brewers have given it the name wine because it has a very high original gravity leading to a high percentage of alcohol and therefore, like wine, requires a period of maturation.

Before going on to brewing Barley Wine we should discuss the use of cereals further.

It is the name Barley Wine that has, in my opinion, caused confusion in the ranks of homebrewers and winemakers in the whole field of using cereals or grain in brewing and winemaking and this covers barley, wheat, maize oats, rice and any other cereal. None of them will make any contribution to the fermentable matter in a brew unless they have been malted, as only then

119

will they convert with hot water to sugars. Cereals which have been cooked into the various flaked products, and even though their starch cells have been exploded, are also of no use in brewing used alone. It is *essential* that they are used in conjunction with a malt mash or a diastatic malt extract so that the enzymes of either will convert their starch into sugars.

I still see some curious beer recipes and only recently read in a homebrewing magazine of a writer boiling toasted bran with his hops. The beer eventually drank well but it took months to clear. I am not surprised. Brewers go to great trouble so that all starch is converted to fermentable sugar but here is a recipe actually ensuring a starch-filled brew. Try boiling bran flakes and then test for starch with iodine. It goes brilliant blue immediately!

On the problem page, one anxious winemaker was having trouble with the fermentation of his wheat wine. Again, I am not surprised. The free starch of unmalted or unconverted cereals is a trouble-making fermentation inhibitor. The enzymes of the yeast will reduce the starch problem over a very long period but I am unable to see the sense of deliberately adding difficulties in the way of starch haze and poor fermentability to beer or wine.

These grain wines have apparently been made, as recipes appear in every winemaking book I have looked at. These recipes, however, use for every pound of barley or wheat a pound or so of raisins and about three pounds of sugar. It is the raisins and sugar which produce the fermentation and presumably the barley is there for the flavour, which I consider to be minimal, and its only further contribution is unwanted starch, with its attendant trouble.

Most recipes require the grain to be 'softened' overnight in water. This will probably ensure a fine collection of lactic and other bacteria and wild yeast in the later must! Other recipes suggest boiling the barley or wheat to start; this would gelatinise the starch and produce a mixture whose only real use would be as an adhesive for wallpaper!

I am sure winemakers have made acceptable wines with unmodified grain but I feel it is the other ingredients that have made the wine and, over a long period, overcome the fault of using unmalted cereal; I would eradicate them from recipes and would suggest that where a pound of barley, wheat or maize is included this be replaced with one pound of pale malt grain, mixed with water at 150°F, or one pound of light malt extract and there will be no trouble with fermentation or cloudiness.

Let us return to the brewing industry for the brewing of real Barley Wine, made with *malted* barley.

BARLEY WINE

Barley wine is just another beer and like all beers it is fermented from the wort, extracted from mashed malt, which is then boiled with hops. It differs from other beers only in that it is about three times as strong and so requires a slightly different treatment.

I mentioned earlier, when dealing with mashing, that a brewer sometimes takes the first strong runnings from his mash into a small vessel and boils them with hops for his strong barley wine and the rest of the wort ex-mash goes into a larger, weaker boil for his ordinary beers. Most breweries have a barley wine and make it as above, i.e., every so often they take a small amount of strong wort for a barley wine and on that day a smaller amount of normal gravity wort is available from their normal mash quantities.

It has to be done this way as any quantity of mash, fully extracted, will produce a wort of about 1.045 gravity. Barley wines should be from 1.090 to 1.100 gravity, so it will be seen that valuable wort, albeit of low gravity, would be left in the mash if only the first strong wort was used.

FAMOUS NAMES

These strong beers from many breweries rejoice in many names such as Old Ale, Stingo, Bishop's Tipple and many others but usually qualify the name with the addition of "barley wine" on the label. The daddy of them all, I suppose, is the famous Bass No. 1 barley wine which used to be naturally conditioned in the bottle and had an original gravity of 1.110. It is still available and excellent, although it is now filtered and stabilised.

These barley wines are invariably of a dark, rich ruby colour because there is little dilution of wort at this high gravity. Barley wines will also have a high final gravity, as the yeast action is slowed by the alcohol produced and it is difficult to obtain the 1/5th to 1/6th of original gravity that brewers like. A 1.100 original gravity beer would still have a final gravity of about 1.020 even after maturation.

The strength of the fermentation also absorbs the bittering of the hops and therefore while 1½ lb per barrel (36 gallons) is a good hop rate for a 1.045 bitter, a strong beer of 1.100 would require 3½ to 4 lb of hops per 36 gallons for bittering to survive as a "cross flavour" to the malty fullness of the beer.

GOLDEN WINE

Mention must be made of a unique and excellent barley wine of a lighter golden colour, albeit equally as strong as its competitors. It was first brewed 30 years ago by Mr Harold Burkinshaw at Tennant Bros, Exchange Brewery, Sheffield, and called Tennants 'Gold Label'.

The brewery joined the Whitbread group, who marketed the barley wine on a national, and international basis as Whitbread 'Gold Label' barley wine and it is probably and rightly, the best known and liked of all strong beers, because it is a superb barley wine.

The formulation of Gold Label is Whitbread's secret, but we can try to assume how it is brewed. It has a high original gravity of 1.101 and you will find that a bottle of 'Gold Label' has a final gravity of 1.018, which follows a very good fermentation giving an alcohol content of about 11%.

Like all beers, the Gold Label will be a mash of the right amount of the right malt and the wort from this will be boiled with carefully chosen hops. To obtain the pale colour at this gravity would require extremely lightly kilned malt and this would also ensure fairly high enzymic activity remaining in the malt. This, in turn, would help in the low final gravity achieved in such a high gravity beer.

It is possible that they might also use a small proportion of pale No. 1 invert cane sugar in the boil to enhance further the light colour and also assist in the low final gravity, but not too much, or it would thin out the full-bodied flavour. After fermentation, a period of maturation in tank will follow, with final filtration and bottling as the sparkling barley wine so many enjoy.

122

HOME BREW BARLEY WINE

Homebrewing lends itself easily to the brewing of strong barley wines, as original gravity can be increased and, after a rather longer period in the fermenting vessel, the natural conditioning and maturation in bottle or gas-tight keg suits a strong beer admirably and a barley wine can be produced that is every bit as good as the commercial variety.

If the five gallon recipes I have previously given were made up to between two and two and a half gallons, very acceptable dark and light coloured strong barley wines would result. The same could be said by making up with half the suggested water, the various complete homebrew kits on the market.

This is something of an over-simplification because a barley wine really needs extra hops, as we know that the stronger fermentation absorbs a great deal of the necessary bittering to balance the malty fullness of the final beer. The hop rate of a 1.045 gravity bitter should be at least doubled to ensure this when gravity is increased to 1.100.

A common error is to increase gravity by adding large amounts of sugar but this will only give a hard, dry and thin palate and malt and sugar should be increased proportionately. It is better to increase malt rather more than the increase of sugar. Here are two barley wine recipes:–

5 gallons 1.100 gravity
BARLEY WINE
(Mashed malt brew)
   13 lb Pale Ale Malt
   4 lb Sugar
   5 oz Golding Hops
   Sachet of dried yeast *or* **2 oz Brewery yeast**

Crush and mash the malt in 3 gallons of water at 170°F to obtain mash heat of 150°F. Hold for two hours. Sparge with 3 gallons of water at 170°F to wash wort from mash. We have already used more water than the 5 gallon brew, but more sparge might still be necessary to extract the full gravity. The surplus water will have to be evaporated by a long boil of the collected wort. A vigorous boil will evaporate about 1 gallon per hour. Hops and sugar are included in the boil.

Strain out hops, cool to 70°F and ferment as usual. If full gravity is not obtained from the mash, add a sugar solution to increase this. The beer will ferment to about 1.020 in ten days to a fortnight. Let it settle for a further week, then bottle with ½ teaspoon priming sugar per pint and allow to condition and mature.

5 gallons 1.100 gravity
BARLEY WINE
(Malt Extract Brew)
   12 lb Malt Extract
   4 lb Sugar
   5 oz Golding Hops
   Sachet of yeast *or* **2 oz Brewery yeast**

Boil hops in 26 pints of water for one hour. Strain out spent hops. Add 5 or 6 pints of water to the hop liquor and dissolve the malt extract and sugar in this. Boil and simmer for 15 minutes, stirring to avoid burning malt extract. Add to water in fermenting vessel and top up to 5 gallons with water. Cool to 70°F, add yeast and ferment as usual. Final gravity will also be about 1.020; finally, treat as with mashed brew.

CHAPTER 15

Beer Kits

The late Reggie Maudling, when chancellor of the exchequer, will always be looked upon as the patron saint of homebrewing for rescinding in 1963 the need for a five shilling licence to brew at home. Clandestine homebrewing was already becoming popular, but this simple act made it legal, caught the notice of the public and started the expansion of a new trade.

Concentrated extract of malt, malt extract, also made it a fairly simple business to make up a reasonable beer with the numerous recipes which began to circulate in the infant journals of the new hobby through the home beer and winemaking Circles and the new retail outlets specialising in the trade. Malt extract did away with the need to mash grain malt and although the mashing purists of the hobby have always alleged that there is a tang when brewing with extract, this is not so!

The early recipes and methods led to beers with a strange homebrew taste, i.e. it was the incorrect use of materials, not the materials themselves, which gave rise to the myth.

A major national brewery has recently set up several in-house breweries in selected pubs brewing with concentrates and a correspondent to 'What's Brewing', the CAMRA magazine, raised the myth once more of non-mashed brews. A spokesman for the brewery answered this with the fact that taste panels had been set up and hundreds of tasters had failed to pick out the concentrate brews in the samples of mixed commercial mashed brews and extract brews tasted.

Malt extract, therefore, is quite correctly the staple material of homebrewing and the keen homebrewer likes to make up his beers with favourite hops and other lesser adjuncts. But as the trade grew, it was not long before the malt extract manufacturers came

125

along with ready-hopped malt extracts. A malt extract factory is in all respects similar to a brewery and the wort ex-mash tun has hops or hop extract added and is then concentrated to a syrup.

Then followed specific types of hopped extract and, by using different grain malts in their mashes and different hops and rate of hopping, a range of types became available such as concentrated bitter wort, stout wort, pale ale and lager wort. These are still available and are probably the best buys for the homebrewer when bought in, say, a 14 lb or 28 lb pail and the brewer can decide on a brew of his choice, adding adjuncts if desired and a little sugar and yeast obtained from the homebrew shop.

It was inevitable that these hopped worts would be packed into cans as complete homebrew kits to brew a specific number of pints, stated on a smart label, with a sachet of yeast and full instructions for brewing included under a plastic cap. They look smart and eyecatching; at this stage the marketing of homebrew kits became a professional operation and there is no doubt that it is the various beer kits which have caused the growth of homebrewing into an industry with a current retail value of about £17 million per annum and still growing.

THE KITS

Beer kits have proliferated into a bewildering choice for the homebrewer, with ever brighter and more attractive labels to tempt him, and it can be said that they all make up to very reasonable beers. There is a great deal of commercial 'cut and thrust' about whose concentrated wort is contained under the colourful label. There are seven manufacturers of malt extract in the UK and all are engaged in the supply of homebrew.

Four of these manufacturers have identifiable homebrew kits and materials which are retailed under their own names. The other three prefer to remain anonymous, although the largest of these has recently acquired a well-known established homebrew range of kits. All seven manufacturers compete vigorously to supply in bulk to the many packers of homebrew kits marketed under various brand names. Five of the manufacturers who have canning facilities also pack and label various brands ranging from national names to small retailers' own labels.

126

VALUE OF KITS

It will be seen that, although there is a wide variety of kits available, there is a limited amount of supplies of basic ingredients and it might well be that two or more brands can be the same except for the label. But it is also true that a packer of a major brand will require a concentrate to his specification.

The homebrewer should know, however, that there is little difference in the qualities of the contents of his beer kit. There are no contents of any kit which are stronger or weaker than any other. All malt extracts are concentrated to within a point or so of 80% solids and this holds good for the various beer types available. A dark beer will have some coloured malt in its make up and less hopping. A stout will have roast barley or malt in the wort produced for concentration and a lager will be produced from very pale lightly cured malt with Continental hops included. Weight for weight, they will all yield the same amount of beer at the same gravity.

The true value of a beer kit is therefore the weight of hopped malt extract of its contents and this is stated on the label and allows the purchaser to compare the price with a kit with similar weight of contents.

5 GALLON KITS

Homebrewing seems to have settled down to a brew of five gallons and this matches the capacities of the many fermenting vessels available and, more important, the numerous 5-gallon kegs on the market. The majority of beer kits conform to this and state on the label "to make 40 pints" or five gallons and the most universal 5-gallon kits are those containing 1.5 kg (3.3 lb) of hopped concentrated extract.

These kits, with 2 lb of sugar added, will make 40 pints of beer at an original gravity 1.036, no more, no less, and you do not get 40 pints of extra-special super beer! It is a reasonable gravity and about equal to ordinary pub beer, but not the best. Since metrication, the 1 kg (2.2 lb) bag of sugar is sometimes used and this increases the gravity to 1.038 but the sugar proportion is beginning to get high and will thin out flavour.

In this category of 5-gallon kits, I notice two kits contain 1.42 kg (3.13 lb) and probably rely on the 1 kg bag of sugar to achieve a reasonable gravity; one kit is available with 1.7 kg (3.75 lb) which with 2 lb of added sugar would produce 40 pints of beer approaching 1.040 gravity and getting into the realm of a pub best bitter.

Variations on these 1.5 kg kits include "extra strong" and "gravity 45" and these are simply achieved by brewing 30 pints instead of 40. You can only get more beer, weaker, or less beer stronger, from a given quantity of concentrate. I do not advise adding more sugar than recommended as, although gravity is increased, the balance between malt and sugar is changed and body or fullness will be lost. Beer is brewed from malt, not sugar.

SPECIAL 5 GALLON KITS

I know of five special 40 pint beer kits and they all contain 1.8 kg (4 lb) of hopped concentrate and, in consequence, are more costly than the 1.5 kg kits. Beer kits tend to sell on how much beer they make and not on how good it is – "Why pay more for only the same 40 pints?" Brewers who think this would be wrong, for these special kits make a very much better and stronger 40 pints.

The 4 lb of malt concentrate also gives a better malt to sugar ratio, closer to commercial brewing practice and leads to a strong, commercial-flavoured beer. A 4 lb kit with 2 lb added sugar will give an original gravity of 1040–1041; with 1 kg (2.2 lb) sugar, the gravity will be 1043–1044 and one of these kits recommends adding 2½ lb of sugar which will give a gravity of 1045–1046. Another of these special kits includes a phial of isomerised hop extract for adjusting bitterness after fermentation, a practice which has been widely adopted in recent years by commercial brewers.

OTHER KITS

There are many other kits, usually for smaller quantities of beer, and there are several available where the malt extract has been dried to powder form. Again with these, the criterion is the weight of malt extract supplied and remembering that malt extract as a syrup is 80% solids, the dry version has had the 20% water dried out and therefore 20% less by weight of dry gives the same gallonage and gravity as in the liquid state.

PRICES

I will not give current specific prices of kits, as these continually fluctuate and some brands will have applied inflationary costs of raw materials and labour and others might still be holding for a time. Special offers also confuse the picture, but the price of kits and what you get for your money does appear to be chaotic. There is one 1.5 kg (3.3 lb) kit that for over a year has had a lower retail price than others. It contains as good a concentrated malt and hop syrup as others and I have taken it as a basis for comparison with the price of other completely similar kits.

Of these others, one costs 22% more in one store and 32% more in another! Another 1.4 kg kit, after a correction for weight, costs 24% more. A well-known brand at 1.5 kg is 29% more in one store and 39% more in another and one multiple store offers a 1.7 kg (3.75 lb) kit which appears to be good value but when corrected for weight is in fact, 5% above our basic kit. The 1.42 kg (3.13 lb) kit sells at the same price as the basic kit, but when corrected for weight is 5% above this in one store and in another 30% above the base.

When we look at the special kits with contents of 1.8 kg (4 lb), on a proportional basis they should be about 20% above the price of the 1.5 kg basic, but they range from 20% to 30% above this and attract a premium price as they are undoubtedly premium kits.

It is perhaps unfair to use the current low-priced kit as a comparison, as it is holding this price for a period to capture a larger share of the market and will undoubtedly come into line with others in the long run, but the homebrewer should always consider weight of contents against price.

METHODS OF USE

Beer kits are very simple to use and carry full instructions to make successful brews. Usually, the contents are dissolved in a given amount of hot or boiling water and this hot solution is made up to the required gallonage in the fermenting vessel by adding cold water. The contents of kits are reasonably sterile, as the wort from which they are made is usually sterilised before condensation, or the complete can is sterilised by immersion. Some kits therefore only instruct to mix in hot water and others insist on bringing the initial solution of the kit to the boil and simmering for about 15 minutes.

Whatever the instructions say, I would always recommend the boiling procedure. Not only will it make certain of a sterile initial mix before fermentation but *all* malt wort when boiled further will throw out and coagulate protein matter which has a very significant bearing on eventual clarity of the final beer.

The yeast supplied with most kits usually makes an initial "fluffy" head, which sinks to the bottom of the brew and continues to work from there. It is essential to keep the fermentation covered when initial gassing of the brew has finished. During the gassing period, the beer is protected, but after this an exposed surface of beer is liable to infection from airborne sources and more homebrews are infected and spoilt from exposure to air than from any other cause.

With a little care, most homebrew kits nowadays make a very palatable and enjoyable drink.

CHAPTER 16

My Standard Brew

I have spent 47 years in the brewing industry and in the last 15 have been closely associated with the homebrewing trade and formulated, designed and marketed a well-known range of home-brew kits and concentrates of various types of beers, lagers, stouts and barley wines.

During this latter period I have always brewed at my home the types of kit to be put on the market so that my brew could be assessed with similar trial brews in the quality control department of the company.

Since retiring I have regularly brewed three 5-gallon brews, in close succession, every two months, and have long ago settled for my Standard Brew, which is a best bitter of 1.045 original gravity. I am pleased to say that it is widely praised by my friends and, in my opinion, is one of the best beers I have tasted in all my years in the trade, commercially produced or home brewed. It is a simple beer, and beer should be simple; I have stressed throughout my notes on brewing that all that is necessary in a good beer is the fermentation of wort from malted barley (malt) and, perhaps, some sugar, balanced by the flavour and bitterness of hops.

I do *not* use any flaked barley, flaked maize or wheat flour "because the commercial brewer uses them", because in the main these and other materials are used to lower production costs, have no real merit and are used very much on the basis of "how much dare we use without a noticeable drop in beer quality?"

My main material therefore is malt and the question is whether to mash grain malt or use concentrated extract of malt (malt extract). I have used both methods and have decided on malt extract, much, I expect, to the horror of the devotees of mashing. I have previously stated that when a good malt extract is diluted and boiled with hops, the result is equal to wort ex-mash tun and beer

131

taste panels have been unable to distinguish beers from either method.

The bonus for malt extract, of course, is simplicity and the elimination of the "messing about" with mashing, but I agree that there is great interest and satisfaction to be obtained from mashing. However, grain malts available are variable in quality and beers produced are consequently variable in strength and quality. Malt extract gives me the same result time after time.

Looking back on my records of 15 consecutive standard brews, they have all fermented to an exact pattern and produced identical beers.

My recipe is, for five gallons:

STANDARD BITTER
1.045 gravity
4 lb Malt extract
2½ lb Granulated sugar or invert sugar
2½ oz Golding hops
2 oz Magnesium sulphate (Epsom Salts)
1½ tsp Caramel
2 oz fresh brewery yeast or 1 sachet beer yeast

It will be seen that the recipe differs only slightly from the malt extract and sugar 1.045 gravity beer previously described, in that the malt extract has been reduced to 4 lb and the sugar increased to 2½ lb. It is a larger sugar ratio than I would advise for a mashed brew but I have found that the rather full 'maltiness' of the extract at this gravity is diluted by the sugar to a well balanced, hoppy bitter.

Method:

Put the hops free (not in a bag) with 28 pints of water into a large boiling vessel and boil vigorously for one hour; the 2 oz Epsom salts are added at the beginning of the boil. Brewers need have no fear of these salts as they are 'lost' in the 5 gallon brew!

When the boil has been going for ten minutes, take out 2 pints of the water and put aside for later inclusion in the brew. – Strain out any hops and return them to the boil. Hop 'aroma' will be retained in the 2 pints, which would be boiled away in the main bulk where the objective is extracting the bittering alpha acids and resins from the hops. The recipe contains rather less hops than some I have seen, but my rate is normal brewing practice for this gravity of beer and the separate one hour boil gives the necessary efficient extraction.

After one hour, about 10 pints of water will have evaporated away and the now spent hops can be filtered out with a nylon strainer.

Dissolve the malt extract and sugar into the remaining hopped liquor and bring this to the boil, stirring to avoid burning the extract. Boil vigorously for 15 minutes to achieve the 'hot break' and coagulation of malt protein, which contributes so much to later clarity. The 1½ tsp of caramel is added to this boil. I add this only because I use a light coloured malt extract.

Two or three minutes before ending the boil of malt extract and sugar, add the 2 pints of hop water previously set aside and this will give a pleasant hop aroma to the final beer. The full extraction of the main amount of hops in the one hour boil is the key factor in giving this beer a good head and head retention. Cool the boiled wort (covered) in a sink of cold water for about half an hour, then pour into the fermenting vessel in which about 10 pints of water has been added. Top up with water to the 5 gallon mark, adding yeast at the same time, but be sure the temperature is about 65° to 70°F before yeast is added.

I am lucky in that a local brewery gives me a jar of yeast for my beer. It is tricky to manage, as it produces a large crop and is very flocculent and has to be roused back into the beer twice a day; at gravity 1.010 the yeast crop has to be skimmed off. A final close head is formed and fermentation stops at 1.008.

I have another brew ready for 2 oz of the skimmed yeast and a third brew will have yeast from the second brew. My three 5-gallon brews are spread over 12 days. My fermentation with brewery yeast is therefore fairly exposed with rousing and skimming, but this is all right while the beer is gassing. When the skimming of the yeast crop is complete, the beer must be covered and air kept away. When using a sachet of dried yeast, the fermentation should be covered at all times as no great crop will be made and no rousing other than rocking the covered beer is necessary. This yeast will also ferment this beer to a stop position of 1.008.

RACKING, PRIMING AND FINING

Allow the covered beer to settle out for two or three days in the fermenting vessel and then it may be bottled or kegged. I use and recommend the use of finings. The beer will clear itself but the difference between 'bright' and 'starbright' is worth the trouble of fining. Use 2 oz of Isinglass gel finings, dissolved in a pint of the beer and when bottling use 1/40th (½ fl oz) of this in each pint bottle, plus ½ tsp of sugar per pint to give secondary condition in the bottle. Do not be afraid of the 1.008 remaining gravity. Only the ½ teaspoon of sugar will ferment to give condition. It is much easier to bottle when the fermenting vessel has a tap at the bottom to which a polythene tube can be fitted to lead into the bottle and fill from the base without fobbing.

KEGGING, PRIMING AND FINING

I keg my beer and for this an absolutely gas tight keg is essential and I recommend a float take-off in the beer to take beer from the top. Beer takes some time to clear to tap level, but is clear in days at the top. The well-known white round keg suits me admirably and I have had three in use for two years without any trouble. The two plates, which are drawn together either side of a grommet, seal perfectly and the nut and bolt which does this incorporates a safety valve and valve for admitting CO_2 gas if needed.

Before kegging my beer, I draw off one pint, gradually dissolving 2 oz of Isinglass gel in this, and also dissolve 5 oz of sugar in one pint of water and boil this briefly.

Before filling the clean and sterile keg I first fill it with CO_2 gas. Assemble the empty keg and inject gas from a gas cylinder for about one second, through the valve. Then open the keg again by removing the cap or plates, depending on which type of keg you have. The gas is heavier than air and will remain in the keg. Now place the keg below the fermenting vessel tap, allow the beer to flow into the keg, filling from the bottom with the 'cushion' of gas preventing any air contacting the beer.

During the filling, pour in the solutions of fining and priming sugar. Close the keg firmly – and then I give a very, very brief squirt of gas into the filled keg. I never need any more gas during dispensing over two or three months. The rather high rate of priming sugar (5 oz) ensures secondary fermentation to give long-lasting pressure for dispensing.

With the float take off and using finings the beer is bright after two or three days but will still be young and too sweet because of the priming. In a week or two this will have fermented away, leaving a star-bright, hoppy bitter with a quite exceptional creamy head and, more important, head retention and attractive 'lacing' left on the side of the glass as you enjoy your pint.

That, therefore, is my standard brew and may be used as the essential framework and method to produce other types. I have previously said that only slight changes are necessary in the basics to produce different types. Strength may be altered up or down by adding or subtracting, but keep the ratio of materials balanced. Take out ½ lb sugar and replace with a ½ lb crystal malt, use only 2 oz of hops and you will have a 'luscious', strong mild ale. Again, take out 1 lb of sugar and put 1 lb of black malt or roast barley in the boil and you will have a fine stout. Keep material quantities the same but use very pale malt extract and Hallertau hops and a strong lager type beer will result.

The permutations are numerous but do keep to the method. The separate vigorous free hop boil and the boil of extract and sugar in the hop water is the essential key to the superb head and clarity of the final beer.

CLEAN AND STERILE

I have never had a beer spoiled in over 15 years of homebrewing and neither has the control laboratory in my company and this is due to sensible precautions. The brewing process is simple superficially, but the biology, biochemistry and microbiology which changes barley to malt and malt to malt sugars and the fermentation of these to an alcoholic beverage are complex and even making up and fermenting a beer kit is a 'living' process and not like making instant coffee.

Waiting in the wings, and particularly in the air, are micro-organisms which can spoil and sour your brew. Dissolve a little malt extract in some water and leave it open in a saucer in your super modern kitchen and you will be surprised at the moulds and bacteria which will grow in it from the air.

The homebrewer should therefore use clean and sterile vessels, kegs and bottles and exclude air as far as possible. The homebrewer can achieve reasonable sterility more easily than the older type of large brewery.

I use a typical household bleach "which kills all known germs" to clean up vessels, but be sure to get to nooks and crevices and taps and clean out small deposits of yeast. Rinse this cleaner away very thoroughly; I then give all vessels and utensils a final wash out with 1 tsp sodium metabisulphite per pint of water and let this drain without a further water rinse. Always boil your brew, including sugar, but in my area I treat tap water as sterile and use it unboiled to make up any brew before fermentation.

When the beer is gassing during fermentation, it is reasonably safe from airborne infections but do not allow flat, i.e. non gassing, surfaces of beer uncovered by yeast to be exposed to air, as this is a time when the beer is very vulnerable to airborne infection. This would almost certainly be lactic bacteria and wild yeasts, which will reduce the pH of the beer, making it more acid and eventually sour. In this condition, the beer is ready for Mycoderma, again an airborne infection, to cover the surface with its white waxy film and further increase acidity and sourness. The situation is irreversible and nothing can restore the beer which, while not poisonous, is distinctly unpleasant and should be thrown away.

Sensible and simple precautions will not allow these disappointments to occur and the homebrewer will continue his rewarding hobby without trouble. A good brewer is like a good chef and will derive great enjoyment from adjusting his brew to his own preference by adding a little of this and taking out a little of that until it is just as he wants it. I am just off for a pint of mine.

Good 'ealth!

Above: Add hops to 28 pints of water.

'MY STANDARD BREW'

Below: Boil vigorously for one hour. When the boil has been going for 10 minutes, take out 2 pints of the water and put to one side.

Above: Strain out spent hops and collect hop water.

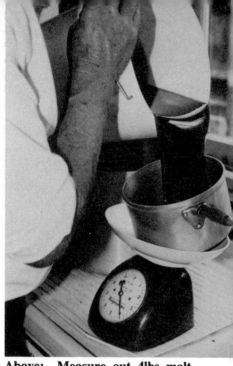

Above: Measure out 4lbs malt extract.

Below: Add malt extract and sugar to the hop water.

Below: Raise to boil and simmer for ten minutes. Keep stirring to avoid any extract burning.

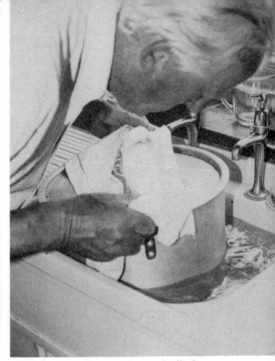

Above: A minute or two before end of boil put back 2 pints of hop water removed at beginning of hop boil.

Above: Cooling the boiled section of the brew.

Below: Adding boiled section of brew to water in fermenting vessel.

Below: Weighing yeast collected from a previous brew.

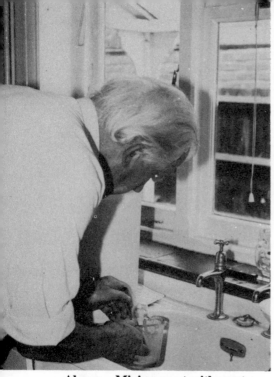 

Above: Mixing yeast with wort.   Above: Adding yeast to brew.

Below: Top up to 5 gallons with water.

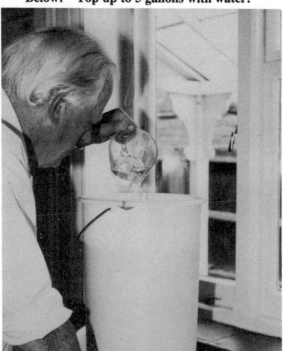

140

INDEX